Gerald Shenk

Also by James Leehan

Pastoral Care for Survivors of Family Abuse

James Leehan

DEFIANT HOPE

Spirituality for Survivors of Family Abuse

Westminster/John Knox Press
Louisville, Kentucky

Unless otherwise noted, scripture quotations are from the New Revised Standard Version of the Bible, copyright © 1989 by the Division of Christian Education of the National Council of the Churches of Christ in the U.S.A., and are used by permission.

Scripture quotations marked JB are from *The Jerusalem Bible,* copyright © 1966, 1967, 1968 by Darton, Longman & Todd, Ltd., and Doubleday & Co., Inc. Used by permission of the publishers.

Portions of chapter 1 appeared in a slightly altered form as "Domestic Violence: A Spiritual Epidemic," in *The Christian Ministry* (May/June 1992). Copyright © 1992 The Christian Century Foundation. Reprinted by permission of *The Christian Ministry.*

The poem on p. 92, "Dear Stranger," by b. f. maiz, is from b. f. maiz, *Dear Stranger,* © 1978 Tuff & Company. Reprinted by permission of the author.

The "Psalms by a Survivor" in Appendix C are reproduced by permission.

Book design by Drew Stevens

First edition

Published by Westminster/John Knox Press
Louisville, Kentucky

This book is printed on acid-free paper that meets the American National Standards Institute Z39.48 standard. ∞

PRINTED IN THE UNITED STATES OF AMERICA
9 8 7 6 5 4 3 2 1

Library of Congress Cataloging-in-Publication Data

Leehan, James.
    Defiant hope : spirituality for survivors of family abuse / James Leehan.—1st ed.
        p.   cm.
    Includes bibliographical references.
    ISBN 0-664-25463-2 (alk. paper)
    1. Victims of family violence—Religious life.   2. Spiritual life.   I. Title.
BL625.9.V52L44   1993
248.8'6—dc20   93-19549

Dedicated to

Robert W. Clarke
1922–1992

Dear friend, campus ministry colleague, and mentor who
modeled for me the sensitivity to others and responsiveness
to human need that enabled me to recognize grown-up
abused children when they appeared in my life.

Contents

Foreword

❚ am pleased to have the opportunity to write the foreword for this book, *Defiant Hope: Spirituality for Survivors of Family Abuse*. Author James Leehan and I first met in 1978 at Cleveland State University where we co-led one of his Grown-Up Abused Children groups. He was (and is!) an exemplary therapist and teacher as well as an ordained minister who has made adult survivors of family violence a special focus of his ministry. His interest began when he recognized many survivors among his students. He then started to organize direct services for survivors, eventually resulting in group offerings throughout Cleveland. His training for group leaders led to the writing of *Grown-Up Abused Children* (coauthored with Laura Wilson Webb), a pioneering book on group treatment for survivors of abuse. His second book, *Pastoral Care for Survivors of Family Abuse*, was written to alert clergy to issues of family violence and to introduce the needs of victims of current abuse and survivors of past abuse in their congregations. He emphasized victims' and survivors' need for compassion and spiritual solace to counter the devastation of abuse. And in this, his third book, he speaks directly to survivors about what he terms the spiritual epidemic of family violence.

The personal and interpersonal consequences of various forms of family violence are now well documented. Abuse within the family perpetrated by those charged with protecting and nurturing is particularly damaging. It undermines individual self-worth and growth and hinders the development of trusting relation-

1

ships. It often creates crises of spirituality. As the spirit is crushed rather than celebrated, profound isolation, alienation, and despair result. A striking finding in retrospective studies of adult survivors is their disillusionment and despair. Many suffer spiritual crises involving a loss of faith and the hope for justice. Many are wary of ever finding a beneficent and just Higher Power. They often live out lives of pain and quiet desperation, without hope of human or divine caring or understanding.

A unique value of this book is its emphasis on the recovery process from a spiritual as well as a religious perspective. Some common religiously-based admonitions to survivors such as "forgive and forget," "to err is human, to forgive is divine," "honor thy mother and thy father," and "turn the other cheek" are challenged as both damaging and potentially dangerous for survivors if applied indiscriminately. Organized religion has tended to minimize the damage of family violence, often encouraging family intactness above all else.

The author emphasizes recovery as a process that is both complex and personal, guided by the hard realities of family violence. Anger, forgiveness, and reconciliation are part of the process, but their meaning and application are not predetermined. Survivors are encouraged to accept their anger and pain as righteous; they are further encouraged to consider forgiveness after achieving solidarity with their pain and to begin with self-forgiveness. Forgiveness of abusive others is dependant, in part, on the *abusers'* ability to acknowledge their damaging actions, to actively repent, and to make reparations to the survivors. But, even if no such behavior is forthcoming, survivors still have the option to forgive if doing so achieves personal peace and restoration.

The ultimate recovery from family violence is the capacity to remain human in the face of and in defiance of the abuse. Many adult survivors lived through the abuse hoping for its cessation and hoping for better. Many, even as small children, nurtured a sense of self consolidated around "not being like them" and not carrying on the legacy of family violence. Their stubborn resilience may have been what allowed them to survive. This book puts their suffering in spiritual perspective and supports their humanity and capacity to move beyond what was done to them.

Who they are is not to be confused with what was done to them. This book offers hope and supports resilience and the human capacity to grow.

CHRISTINE A. COURTOIS, PH.D.
Clinical Director
Center for Abuse Recovery & Empowerment
The Psychiatric Institute of Washington, D.C.

Introduction

This book owes its existence to the initiative of survivors of family violence. My involvement in the field of family violence came about because student survivors at Cleveland State University made their presence known to me and a faculty colleague in the Department of Social Work. Their courage in identifying themselves and expressing their needs resulted in the formation of a Grown-Up Abused Children group. Survivors in the community who heard about the campus group came forward to ask for a similar program. That prompted the writing of *Grown-Up Abused Children* to prepare other counselors to lead such groups.

Many survivors over the years have had the courage to confront me about religious teachings that they thought contributed to family violence and about the responses of some of my clergy colleagues to victims and survivors of family violence. Their comments and criticisms provided the basis for a book on family violence for clergy, *Pastoral Care for Survivors of Family Abuse.* Some survivor friends took the initiative to read it "only because you wrote it." Their response was, "Much of that was helpful. I would not normally read a book addressed to clergy and I'm not real big on that religious stuff, but a lot of what you wrote helps me understand some of my hang-ups. You ought to rewrite it for survivors."

Hence, this book was written. I hope it meets those expectations and responds to the need for a better understanding of how abuse in the family can be challenged by the Jewish and Christian traditions and how those traditions can help individuals confront and resolve the emotional and spiritual problems generated by abuse. I have tried to write this book without resorting to religious and theological jargon and to address the issues in such a way that the spiritual values of the Jewish and Christian traditions can be positive factors even if readers are not willing or able to "buy" the whole religious "package." For good or ill, Jewish and Christian teachings are woven through much of Western culture. They have been used to justify violence; they can also be instruments of peace and sources of healing.

Abuse in families constitutes betrayal and victimization by those who should have been loving caretakers. Personal control, dignity, and worth are stolen. Identity, personality, and spiritual development are distorted. Deep pain and profound physical and psychological wounds are inflicted.

But that does not become the defining reality for all who are abused. Many free themselves from the control of their abusers, regain power over their lives, and begin to affirm their dignity, worth, and identity. They reaffirm their lives, their existence and their rights. They become survivors.

To those of you who have begun that process I say: I salute you and stand in awe of your resilience! While it is true that for many, the road to survival has been long and arduous, you have begun the process of redefining your personality as separate from that of your abuser. The beginning is the most critical step. I congratulate you on the initiatives you have taken and hope that this book will help you continue your growth.

This book is written primarily for those who have experienced abuse in the past and are struggling to overcome its effects. You may have experienced abuse as a child—ten, fifteen, twenty or more years ago—and you are still struggling to overcome the anger, confusion, and frustration that continue to haunt your life. Or you may be a battered woman who is seeking outside help for the first time to break the cycle of violence that has terrorized your life and that of your family. No matter how recently you have experienced abuse, the very fact that you are asking for help has transformed you from a victim into a survivor. Your process of healing has begun.

Although this book has been written primarily for people involved with the Jewish and Christian traditions, it will also have application for others. Even if you are not an active member of a church or synagogue, their teachings permeate much of secular society and may still have an impact on your thinking. Secular social workers, educators, and all persons involved in the helping professions will, I believe, find that the religious values examined and the conflicts around anger and forgiveness are issues for many of their clients.

The opening chapter of this book examines the epidemic proportions of the physical and spiritual health problems of family violence. This section will point out that abuse is not a unique experience but a devastating infection in our whole society. As a survivor you are one among many.

The remaining chapters examine the religious resources of the Jewish and Christian traditions that can promote healing and spiritual growth for survivors. People involved in the recovery movements have long known how critical a strong spirituality is for overcoming the devastation associated with any dysfunction. The dysfunction created by violence in a family is deeply ingrained. Rooting it out requires all the resources that can be marshaled. The aid of trusted counselors can provide invaluable guidance and insight. A deep spiritual life can enhance and enrich the process of growth.

The Jewish and Christian religions have strong spiritual traditions that have often been overlooked by the recovery movements. This book draws on this grand spiritual resource for healing, wholeness, and holiness. It will explore the defiant nature of the virtue of hope that can call forth new possibilities in the face of the devastating sin of family violence and the crushed dreams produced by it. The virtue of anger, which zealously proclaims what is right, will also be examined as well as the toughness of forgiveness that challenges hurt at the same time that it refuses to let past pain control one's present life. The defiant nature of prayer will also be examined as well as prayer as a way to challenge God about the injustices involved in family violence.

A first appendix looks at the religious messages of the Jewish and Christian traditions that bear on families and family violence. Distorted and simplistic interpretations of these teachings have contributed to family violence. These teachings will be reexamined to see whether they can be "redeemed" and how they can become sources of liberation from violence.

A second appendix provides guided meditations specially adapted for survivors, and a third presents contemporary psalms written by a survivor who wishes not to use her name here. These psalms are a student survivor's response to reading the part of the manuscript for this book that deals with the lamentation psalms. She said, "Reading that gave me permission to address God in new ways." She has kindly given me permission to use her work in this book.

Many people deserve thanks for their help and support of this work. Most important is my wife, Angie. She deserves a great vote of thanks not only for her encouragement and her willingness to read and offer suggestions on the manuscript but also for her patience and forbearance for the preoccupation this project has created for me. My daughters, Barbara and Kathy, deserve similar thanks for their patience for any neglect of their needs that this project may have caused.

Other people have read drafts of the manuscript and offered suggestions: Elizabeth Carmichael, Melissa Lawler, Greg McCoy, Margaret Mills, the Reverend Nancy Rich, Diane Schaefer, and Margo Johanna Walsh. David Blumenthal, who holds the Chair of Judaic Studies at Emory University, offered many valuable suggestions and references that have strengthened the Judaic content of the book. Harold Twiss, my editor at Westminster/John Knox Press, deserves a special note of thanks for his recommendations on the organization of the book. I believe his suggestions have made the material more accessible and readable.

The first two sections of chapter 1 appeared in a slightly different format in the May–June 1992 issue of *The Christian Ministry* (Christian Century Foundation). It was entitled "Domestic Violence: A Spiritual Epidemic."

I especially want to thank the members of my various Grown-Up Abused Children groups over the years. Their courage and commitment have inspired me and taught me much about spirituality. Their initiatives have prompted my efforts in this work. I hope its publication will provide them with greater insights and resources for their spiritual development.

1 | The Spiritual Epidemic of Family Violence

Shortly before he retired as United States Surgeon General, C. Everett Koop called family violence the most serious public health issue in the United States. He maintained that it is at epidemic proportions. Battering by spouses is the largest single reason women seek treatment in emergency rooms. Violence in the family is the largest single cause of death for children under the age of five. Koop called on the health care community to train its members to recognize the effects of such violence in its patients and to learn appropriate treatment.

Survivors of family violence certainly appreciate Dr. Koop's concern and are grateful for his call to action. But the violence perpetrated in the very place one should feel safe and secure is also a spiritual health issue. Such violence attacks the very core of life and undermines the foundation on which a spiritual life can be built, and a deep and meaningful relationship to God and other people can be formed. The ability to trust, to have faith in oneself, others, or God is impaired. The anger such violence generates isolates people from others at the same time that it frightens them and destroys any hope for peace of mind.

As a battered wife or an abused child you may have turned to your local religious congregation for help. You may have thought that churches and synagogues were uniquely equipped to respond to this spiritual health crisis. Most congregations build their programming around the family lives of their members. Religious communities have long had an outstanding reputation for commitment to the sanctity of marriage and the sacredness of the family.

You may have gone to your pastor or rabbi for assistance. (Studies indicate that almost thirty percent of battered women turn to clergy in their first effort to seek help. This rate is the same as those who seek help from counselors and is twice as high as the number who seek help from doctors.) However, you may have discovered that not all religious leaders perceive family violence as a spiritual disease. They do not recognize it for the debilitating infection it is and do not bring the full force of their moral and spiritual energies to bear on it. Many clergy, by their own admission, do not take such reports seriously. In some studies clergy report that they often question the reliability of the accounts they receive; they challenge the woman's degree of submissiveness to her husband and do not consider violence a breach of the marriage contract serious enough to justify leaving a husband or seeking a divorce. They acknowledge that they frequently advise women to return to the violent setting that is their family.

If you received such advice, you were sent back into diseased, dangerous, and potentially deadly circumstances, and you were left morally confused, personally degraded, and spiritually abandoned. Your spiritual growth was weakened because your sense of trust and personal worth were undermined. In effect, you were told you were not worth protecting and that it is okay for you to be abused. You were left helpless and hopeless. You were advised to forgive, to forget, and to accept as normal a physically and spiritually destructive environment. The tenets of your faith that were intended to be sources of support and empowerment became tools of your oppression. You were counseled to be submissive to the very people who abuse you. You were told that the suffering inflicted by this violence was redemptive and character building.

If you were a child growing up in a churchgoing home that was also violent, you may have been confronted with an additional problem. When you sought help from your pastor, you may have been faced with someone who knew and respected your parents as regular and devout churchgoers and as valued and effective members of church councils and the community. However, such activities do not preclude the possibility of violence and abuse. All too frequently abusive parents function very effectively and compassionately in the public arena.

If you had such parents and you sought help within your parents' religious congregation, you were probably not believed and were told that the discipline you received was for your own good and that you were experiencing the rod of loving discipline, which was not to be spared. Then you were sent back home with the admonition to honor your father and mother. You quickly learned to keep your pain to yourself and you came to believe that you were not valued or worthy of protection. You were made to feel worthless, helpless, and unloved.

Thus, the responses you received from religious leaders may have compounded the spiritual problems created by your family violence. As a battered woman you may find it difficult to relate to a church that seems to tell you that you are not worth protecting and that your role in life is to submit patiently to violence and degradation. You may not be able to believe in a God who reportedly condones such treatment. As an abused child you may find it difficult to develop a meaningful faith because you could not trust your primary care-givers. You may not identify with a God who is compared in glowing terms to the very person who heaped unprovoked or excessive violence on you.

These spiritual problems are compounded when the religious leaders who embody the teachings and commitments of the religious community imply that what is going on is acceptable. Those religious leaders also indicated that you as a victim were not worth caring about if they told you, "Don't be angry" after you had been beaten, sexually assaulted, and degraded. To deny you such justifiable anger was to say that you were not valued enough to merit righteous indignation for such treatment. When you were told to forgive, forget, and return to often life-threatening environments as if nothing happened and yet your abuser was not challenged to repent or change, you were being told to submit to more of the same. The message was: "You are not valued as a human being." It is little wonder that your spirituality was strained and your inherent sense of justice, fairness, and reason offended when you were asked to accept the notion that the suffering you were enduring was redemptive and character building, yet the religious leaders who advocated that did not seem concerned about reforming the character of your abuser. The source of your suffering went unchallenged.

These are some of the spiritual conflicts you may have encountered as one who suffered from the spiritual health problem of family violence. Your problems originated in the violence of your family, but were frequently compounded by the responses you received from spiritual leaders. Those who ought to have been the source of a cure contributed to the malady instead.

The Healing Process

If you are to heal the devastating disease of family violence that has afflicted you, you need to acknowledge that the violence you experienced in your family may be a significant factor in many of the personal crises you face. You must acknowledge that your lack of faith may be a perfectly natural response to the untrustworthy world you experienced as an abused child, that your anger and frustration are appropriate and healthy responses to the hurt and pain you experienced as an abused wife or that your alcohol and chemical dependency may constitute a desperate attempt to escape or dull the pain of violent rejection by those you loved. If you wish to heal the spiritual scars created by your battering, it is important to recognize the source of the wounds and defiantly challenge the betrayal that has infected your life.

There is an important healing process involved in overcoming this spiritual disease. Merely seeking to forgive and forget is *not* a healing response. Forgetting that abuse occurred is not only dangerous, it is also impossible and spiritually unhealthy. The terrible things that were done to you need to be acknowledged and integrated, along with their effects, into your life. In order to do this you must affirm the justifiable anger you feel and learn appropriate and effective ways of expressing it. Only by experiencing such anger can you arrive at a true "tough forgiveness" and "let loose" the sin that has been inflicted on you. Only by acknowledging that forgiveness is a tough and demanding process for survivor and abuser alike will you overcome the long-term effects of the spiritual disease of family violence. The major concern of this book will be to determine the proper meaning of tough forgiveness and its role in spiritual healing.

Treatment of any disease is only a stopgap, Band-Aid approach to dealing with a public health crisis. As compassionate and caring as treatment may be and as much as pain may be alleviated for those afflicted, it does little or nothing to eradicate the source of the affliction.

To bind up the wounds of family violence, the source of the infection in individual lives and in society must be addressed. The breeding grounds of the disease must be eliminated and every opportunity for the disease to spread must be wiped out.

Unfortunately, some simplistic, incomplete, and distorted interpretations of the Judeo-Christian scriptures have provided some of the breeding ground for the virus of family violence. All too frequently Paul's admonition that wives be subject to their husbands is invoked without acknowledging that it is contained within a passage that also challenges men to be subject to their wives and points out that "mutual accommodation" (a better translation of the Greek than "subjection") is a necessary requirement for any fruitful relationship.

While it is true that children are urged to honor their fathers and mothers and that parents are encouraged to discipline their children, the same scriptures also point out that parents should not provoke their children to anger and that the rod of discipline is to be tempered with gentleness. It should also be remembered that discipline means training or teaching and does not necessarily imply physical punishment. There are many very effective, nonviolent ways to discipline children.

It is true that marriage is a sacred covenant and faithfulness to that covenant is critical for the spiritual growth of all members of the family. However, violence within a marriage constitutes a serious violation of that covenant—more serious than sexual infidelity. Violence destroys the basic trust required for any covenant. It undermines the basis of the relationship and threatens the spiritual development of all members of the family. Children are more apt to be aware of violence between their parents than of their sexual infidelities. In such homes there is also a high probability that the children will be physically attacked; they are certainly psychologically abused by the violence they observe. It must be affirmed that a marriage is sacred only if it is safe and peaceful for all its members.

Your spiritual healing may require that you clearly and explicitly examine these issues. You may need to challenge distorted interpretations of the scriptures that have given you incorrect and harmful conclusions about the rights and roles of women and children in a family and the requirements of the marriage covenant. Those conclusions have created a breeding ground for family violence that may have stifled, maimed, or destroyed much of your spiritual life, as they have for millions of women and children in our society. A conspiracy of silence about family violence, fostered by religious as well as civil leaders, has allowed the disease to flourish undetected. Such a spiritual health problem requires a reexamination of scripture and theology and a commitment to focused prayer and spiritual reflection. Such a process may be essential so that those of you who have already been afflicted can be restored to health and the infection of the next generation can be prevented.

The treatment and prevention of the spiritual infection created by family violence is the focus of this book. Its purpose is to help you, the survivor, understand the implications of what was done to you, analyze the distorted messages you may have been given by the general society as well as the religious community, and gain the spiritual insights and skills that can enable you not only to heal your wounds but to increase "in wisdom and in years, and in divine and human favor" (Luke 2:52).

You Are Not Alone

The prevalence of violence in families is becoming more and more widely recognized. Sensational cases are regularly reported in the media. TV docudramas portray the perils of battered wives. Yet only the most dramatic cases qualify for media coverage. One out of four or five children experience abuse before they are eighteen, and fifty thousand wives are battered annually, according to conservative calculations of reported cases. If the newspapers tried to cover them all, there would be little room for anything else. And despite their best efforts, journalists can't report the distorted sense of self and the world that family violence creates. Their accounts cannot capture the spiritual devastation that accompanies it.

For you family violence was not merely a matter of media interest but also a subject of painful personal concern. Your experience of abuse probably never received public notice or even

attracted the attention of the social welfare agencies designated
to deal with this problem. You may have been threatened and
intimidated by your husband or insulted, ridiculed, frightened,
and neglected by your parents without a blow being struck. Thus,
there was nothing specific to be reported, nothing physical to be
measured, and since there was no evidence, statistically there was
no abuse. But you know very well there was distress, pain, and
anguish. Your life was distorted and crippled. Because your
family was a place of terror rather than security, you needed
consolation, support, and healing, but you received little if any
such encouragement and assistance. You were left to your own
devices to sort out your fear and pain and confusion.

Because there was so little discussion of family violence when
you were growing up or when your husband first began to beat
you, you probably felt you were the only person to whom this was
happening. You perhaps felt you deserved what was happening to
you or that this was the way all families were. You didn't like it,
but you accepted the abuse as inevitable. You kept your thoughts,
feelings, and frustrations to yourself. As Margaret Hyde puts it so
poignantly in her book title, you learned to "cry softly" for the
pain you experienced (1986). You may well be one of millions of
women who were physically battered and are struggling to
rebuild their lives. You may be among the millions of adults, both
men and women, who experienced abuse as children and are now
struggling to overcome the effects of that violence on your lives.
You are not alone and this book is written for you.

You may also be among the thousands of people who are
coafflicted. You were never abused, but you observed it in your
family or are living with persons who are emotionally or psychologically handicapped because of the violence they experienced.
You may be the friend or spouse of someone who was abused.
Learning of their past abuse may have made you uneasy or
confused. You may wonder how you can help them deal with the
pain and confusion of their abusive background. You may be
confused about how to respond to the conflicting, confusing, and
downright aggravating ways they act. You understand that their
frustrating behaviors stem from their experiences in a violent
family, but no matter how hard you try, you can't sort out all the
conflicting messages. You, too, are not alone, and I hope this book
will also be helpful to you.

The statistics tell you that past and present victims of family violence are easy to find. They exist throughout our community. They are found in every stratum of society, in every educational and professional group, in every religious congregation. However, statistics are of little consolation when you are struggling with your personal pain, anger, and sense of worthlessness. They mean little when you are confronted with the misdirected anger of your spouse or the unexplained and uncontrollable anguish of a friend. Quoting statistics does not make you feel any less alone, nor does it solve any problems. Even if past abuse is acknowledged as part of the problem, well-meaning friends may ask what difference it makes today. After all, it happened ten years ago. Isn't it a matter of the past and best forgotten? Isn't "forgive and forget" a good principle?

That was certainly my attitude for most of my life and ministry. Then late in the fall of 1977, Elizabeth Carmichael, a faculty member in the Department of Social Services, told me that when she had taught a section on child abuse in one of her classes, a number of students approached her privately to confide that they had been victims of abuse. She was struck by the fact that each of them said they had never shared this experience with anyone before, and they each identified similar problems in their present life that they thought were unique. The problems all seemed to be connected to the fact that they had been abused.

Her account sparked memories of similar stories I had recently heard from some of my individual counselees. After several sessions, they had shared with me the fact that they had been abused as children. Each had revealed this information with some trepidation because they had never talked about it before. They were ashamed of what had happened and they felt that they were betraying their parents. The kind of problems that these students identified were similar to those shared by the social service students.

Elizabeth and I discussed our experiences at some length and determined that one of the major issues for the students was a profound sense of isolation. They had never told their stories to anyone before, and all felt that they and their problems were unique. Possibly, we concluded, they would receive some help from being together and sharing their stories with one another. The students were contacted individually and asked if they would be willing to participate in such a group. Most, but not all, were willing to give it a try.

Early in January 1978 the first Grown-Up Abused Children group convened at Cleveland State University. All present, including the leaders, were extremely nervous. What would happen? What would we talk about? We had agreed to meet for an hour and a half. Was there enough to fill the time? The first introductions were vague and general, but as the more courageous of the group shared bits and pieces of their abusive pasts, the level of anxiety dropped and the eagerness to share with one another increased. They realized that finally they were with people who would believe their stories. Finally there were people who understood what had happened, how terrible their childhoods had been, and what distress, confusion, anger, and frustration that abuse had created in their lives. Here were people who would not challenge them to prove their stories. Here were people who would not be horrified to hear their accounts of violence and abuse. In fact, they could match them story for story. It was finally all right to talk about what had happened. They would be heard and understood, believed and supported.

Two hours later we had to call the meeting to a halt. In those two short hours a group had been born and relationships had been established in ways most of those present had never before experienced. For the next seven months the group met faithfully every week. It was discontinued with great regret. Graduations and new jobs forced people to move in different directions.

Each year since then a similar group has met at Cleveland State University. Minimal advertising has produced more than the eight-person maximum for each group. After a few years, requests for memberships were received from the wider community. Volunteer leaders were recruited from the social service and mental health communities. Soon a network of six to eight groups were meeting weekly throughout the Greater Cleveland community. Unfortunately, an extensive waiting list of prospective members still exists.

I learned from all this that there are a tremendous number of survivors of family violence in our city—and Cleveland is hardly unique. These survivors are very real, bright, creative, and talented people who, despite their apparent successes, are suffering tremendous guilt and pain and are struggling to create the healthy lives their families denied them. There are persons living and working in cities throughout this country who are carrying on normal lives as productive members of society, but who are also living with the anguish of betrayed trust and lost childhoods. And they have no one with whom to share their pain.

What you as a survivor need is understanding and support as you try to understand your past. You need education and training so you can unlearn the behaviors that you know so well but are so destructive and counterproductive. Then you can learn new ways to relate to the people around you. To be more specific, you need to learn when to use the highly developed self-protection skills that have become ingrained in you by your abuse experience and when you can be open and trusting with the people around you. In many ways, you need to get back in touch with your abuse experience in order to sort out what aspects of it are appropriate for the real world you live in today. In the words of the subtitle of Dr. Ray Helfer's book, *Childhood Comes First* (1984), you as a survivor need "a crash course in childhood for adults," the opportunity to learn the basic life-skills you were never taught or were mistaught as children. You also need a crash course in religion and spirituality that confronts the distorted religious teachings, scriptural interpretations, and spiritual formation your abusive family provided and some clergy may have reinforced.

It is to this process that the rest of the book is dedicated. My contention is that our society and our churches and synagogues have too long overlooked the psychological and spiritual needs of adult survivors of family violence. Many critically important programs now exist to end abuse, to protect children and battered women, and to help abusive parents end their mistreatment of their children, but more are needed to examine and treat the long-term effects of abuse. At a time when society is recognizing the prevalence of family violence, it is important that it also recognize and treat the effects of abuse on those from previous generations, those whose suffering was unrecognized or ignored in the past. What happened in unholy families must be recognized if it is to be overcome. Churches and synagogues can play a critical role in this task. If the infections and wounds of family violence are treated, they can be cured. When the spiritual distortions and debilities are examined and corrected health, wholeness, and holiness can result.

2 | Restoring Spirituality: Defiant Hope

If neither holiness nor wholeness existed in your home, the search for peace of mind and a meaningful and empowered spiritual life was likely very difficult. Much traditional spiritual teaching focuses on overcoming evil and sin, on controlling one's pride. As a survivor you do not need an emphasis on evil and sin—you have had more than enough of that. As a victim, you were constantly told how wicked and bad you were. As a survivor you are struggling to overcome that image. You do not need to be told to suppress your pride. You have so little self-confidence that pride is not a deadly sin; it is an impossibility. Your self-esteem is too damaged for you to suffer from arrogance. You do not need lectures on asceticism and mortification. You have been sufficiently humiliated and mortified by members of your family.

At its basic level, spiritual life is communication between God and humans. Spirituality is the process of recognizing and fostering the connections between what is most essential in ourselves and what is both inherent to our world and transcendent to it (God). It involves accepting the gifts of creation within us and around us, celebrating their value and appreciating and employing them within the total context of God's love. Spirituality is the process of humans learning to "know fully" even as we "have been fully known" so that "faith, hope, and love abide" (see 1 Cor. 13:12, 13).

Spirituality for survivors must begin with identifying their own essential value. It needs to focus on growth and empowerment, on identifying and affirming gifts and strengths, and appreciating and celebrating the joy and fulfillment that are possible through the grace of the God of love. It must be based on a recognition of and commitment to achieving the blessings and promises offered to all by a loving Creator God. Such a spirituality for survivors will demand a defiant rejection of the negativity and humiliation that marked their home lives. It will require challenging all the negative messages, some possibly with religious overtones, that have formed their image of themselves.

The renowned authority on such an approach to spirituality, Henri J. M. Nouwen, has described spiritual life as a movement from loneliness to solitude, hostility to hospitality, and illusion to prayer. Solitude, hospitality, and prayer are not ends in themselves but means to the fullness of life in and with God. The goal is a new life that enables one to love oneself, others, all of creation, and the Creator with joy and fulfillment. Solitude, hospitality, and prayer are steps along the way to new life, to a holiness that gives wholeness to life and grants peace.

Survivors, People of Hope

Nouwen's first step in spiritual growth is the movement from loneliness to solitude, from being uncomfortable and anxious within oneself to inner peace. A key impediment to progress in spiritual growth is fear. Nouwen says, "the roots of loneliness . . . find their food in the suspicion that there is no one who cares and offers love without conditions, and no place where we can be vulnerable without being used" (1975, 16). For you, as a survivor of family violence, that suspicion was confirmed in your family from infancy. Your well-founded fear of those closest to you instilled loneliness, created isolation, and imposed silence.

Yours is not an isolation in silence that fosters reflection, but one filled with the noise of anxiety, depression, and frightening images. Nouwen says that to turn loneliness into solitude one must love the questions life has presented and pay attention to the innermost self worthy of love (1975, 28). However, your innermost self has been declared unworthy of love and the questions of life have challenged the very value of your existence.

Nouwen maintains that "the beginning of healing is in the solidarity with the pain" of life (1975, 43). For you, this pain is physically real and personal. To confront it means you must confront all the distrust and suspicion, even of yourself, that you were so effectively taught throughout your life. Since this suspicion and distrust is so deeply ingrained, it is a difficult and frightening task. Therefore, the initial focus of your spiritual growth must be on calling forth your hope in the face of hopelessness.

To achieve spiritual healing, you need to affirm the possibility for new life. You must be convinced that you can be saved "from the hands of those who enslaved [you]," you can "break the bars of [your] yoke," and "be secure on [your] soil [your home]" (see Ezek. 34:27). Because of your experiences this does not come naturally. The common blessings of life (security, acceptance, and love) are for you "as yet unseen." Justice and peace have never reigned for you, even in the home that ought to have been your source of comfort. You are still seeking a home in which you can reside in safety. In a paradoxical way this makes you a person of hope.

In his book *Hope Within History*, Walter Brueggemann points out that hope is the virtue primarily of those who do not possess the blessings and power of this world that make one satisfied and complacent. Hope is the virtue of those who see the imperfection of the present, who recognize the fear, insecurities, and inequalities that exist, and who work for a new order of things. This recognition of imperfection and its articulation are critical aspects of hope because *"hope emerges among those who publicly articulate and process their grief over their suffering"* (1987, 84, emphasis his).

To grow to your full spiritual stature, you as a survivor must articulate your pain because "the first enemy of hope is *silence, civility, and repression"* (Brueggemann 1987, 88, emphasis his). To speak your pain is to break out of loneliness and believe that the questions and anxieties of life can be resolved. To speak your pain is the first step toward forgiveness and healing. It is the first step toward experiencing faith that "is the assurance of things hoped for, the conviction of things not seen" (Heb. 11:1). Achieving this assurance is not easy because it means allowing yourself to be flooded with feelings of shame and exposure and then articulating your suffering, and experiencing solidarity with your pain. Having an "empathic other" with whom to share this pain is important. The act of sharing pain, of challenging the silence and repression, of opening oneself to the potential for love and support when feeling the most unloveable is the ultimate act of faith (trust) and the beginning of hope.

Remembering in Order to Recover

Solidarity with one's pain may seem like an irrational and even unhealthy goal. None of us likes to remember painful times in our lives. And when speaking about family violence there are many reasons to deny and forget. You were told not to talk about what was done to you in the privacy of your home. To do so would create tremendous guilt because you feel you are betraying your parents. You also may not want to identify yourself as abused. You may not wish to call what happened to you abusive. To do so imposes a label you prefer to avoid. It evokes too many painful memories you have labored long and hard to erase. It also generates too much anxiety about how others might perceive you. It is presumably easier to ignore what happened to you.

Many times Grown-Up Abused Children group members have reported that counselors have told them, "Don't tell me about the abuse you've experienced. I don't want to talk about it. It happened ten years ago. Forget it and go on." You may have had the same experience. Counselors denied the relationship of your past abuse to your present problems and they refused to discuss it, even though this issue was the single most pressing concern for you as a survivor. You may have been told by religious counselors to "forgive and forget." Such advice discourages solidarity with one's pain.

Some prospective group members also have said that the reason they want to join the group is so they can "learn how to forget about their past abusive experience." I tell them that if they are committed to that agenda, they have come to the wrong place because one of the goals of the group is to help them remember the past, sometimes specific incidents and sometimes in great detail. It is necessary to recall incidents in order to see their relationship to present behaviors and problems. Furthermore, they can never really forget what happened no matter how hard they try. Unfortunately, it is part of their lives and there is no way they can change that fact. There is no way to erase it and to try is counterproductive because it takes too much energy. Great amounts of psychic energy must be expended to repress anger or block memories. Many survivors report great increases in personal energy when repressed feelings and incidents have been remembered.

You may, on the other hand, find it difficult to identify what happened to you as abusive. It is too painful for you to acknowledge the reality of what happened. Or you may have totally blocked the experience from your memory. It is not uncommon for survivors, even those who remember and admit what happened to them, to have long periods in their lives (even several years) for which they have no recollections. Certain aspects of their abusive backgrounds were too painful. They blocked their memories as a means of self-preservation, as a way to maintain a semblance of normalcy in their chaotic lives. These were natural and necessary reactions to an unnatural and violent environment.

Unfortunately, such denial does not block the effects of abuse. Such forgetfulness is often counterproductive because it may result in merely disguising the issue. Even if you as a survivor successfully block your memories—even whole periods of your life—that really only changes the focus of the problem. Your concerns move from anger about abuse to unfocused, seemingly irrational anxiety, from fear of your father or abusive husband to distrust of all men. You may successfully block your memory, but you generate other problems in the process, problems whose sources are unknown and, therefore, difficult to control and resolve.

Even so, the purpose of the Grown-Up Abused Children program is not to dwell on the past or exchange horror stories. The starting point of discussion is a current problem. Many persistent problems of the present have their origin in past abusive experiences. These problems are often learned responses to violent experiences ineffectively or inappropriately applied to the present. Excessive anxiety, raging fears, and uncontrollable behaviors are frequently products of a violent past. The Swiss psychotherapist J. Konrad Stettbacher describes these behaviors as latent reactions that, out of a sense of self-preservation, have become "rigid and ready to spring into action at any time" (1991, 18). The group will help identify the experiences of the past that have connections with or similarities to present difficulties.

These connections are not always immediately clear. Often group members have come into a meeting visibly upset. When asked to share what is bothering them, they say, "It is not appropriate for this group." After being convinced to discuss it with the group and letting the members determine whether the material is relevant, they frequently discover that a present problem with a boyfriend, husband, child, friend, or schoolwork has a connection to their past experience. Part of the reason for the difficulty, or part of the reason they are unable to resolve a fairly minor dilemma, stems from the similarity of this event to their past or anxieties they have carried over from past events. Seeing the connections makes it easier to resolve the problem.

Through seeing connections, by achieving solidarity with your pain, you may also discover that identifying connections between past incidents and the present will help determine what aspects are affecting your present situation. Usually this process of recollection can be done in a straightforward manner. Simple discussion of past and present events can identify similarities and differences.

At other times the process may become more complicated because your memory has blocked significant details about past experiences. Then the process may be more time-consuming. If you have only vague recollections of related past events, it may be helpful to close your eyes and try to put yourself back into the situation, remembering as many details as possible about the room, the clothes you were wearing, exterior noises, anything that will help you "relive" the experience.

It may be helpful to keep a journal in which you record what bits and pieces of memory you do have. Since memory is essentially a reconstructing of the past, collecting all the bits in one place can eventually give you enough to begin construction. You can progressively gather enough pieces to build a complete picture, just as when one assembles a jigsaw puzzle. The discovery of one piece provides clues to how other pieces fit. You may have to begin from the outside with the simpler pieces that are flat on one side and work inward, but you can eventually construct a total picture.

This is not a process you should undertake alone; it can become very painful. Often, you may begin to recall particularly unpleasant aspects of the event. You may recall for the first time that sexual abuse was involved or that there were other members of your family present who did not protect you. You will need support at this difficult time, but it is extremely important for you to deal with these painful recollections. Often such unremembered, blocked aspects of an experience hold the key to your healing.

However, such keys may not be immediately available. There may be no recollections of past events available for whole periods of your life. In such cases it is best simply to acknowledge the possibility of blocked incidents, recognize that such memory gaps exist, and let whatever memories you do have simmer until new images and connections are generated. Do not force the issue or blame yourself for blocking your recollections. Trying to force things simply increases anxiety, reinforces low self-esteem, and makes the process more difficult. Simply acknowledge the possibility and leave it for relaxed reflection. Periodically you may want to focus on the issue to see if anything new surfaces. If nothing does, relax and leave it for another time.

Remembering the Sins of the Family

As you try to recall your past, the critical question is, What are you trying to reconstruct? What factors of your family life do you need to examine? Much of your past was so painful that you may prefer not to remember it. What should you look for to determine whether your family experience was outside the norm?

Our society has always had an ample supply of ideal families to emulate—Ozzie and Harriet of the 1950s, the Huxtables of the '80s. In those families the children seldom needed to be punished and when they did they were never swatted or spanked, they were never yelled at or ridiculed or put down. The punishment was moderate and always fit the crime. Ozzie and Harriet and Cliff and Claire were perfect parents and the ideal couples. Even when they got frustrated or felt out of sorts, they still knew all the proper child-rearing techniques and practiced them perfectly. They always managed to settle their disputes in a peaceful and reasonable manner. A hand was never raised in anger and neither a harsh nor a discouraging word was ever uttered—and the sky was not cloudy all day. Such families were truly the kind that could be described as "sacred." They were the kind of family that fit the glowing descriptions provided in church on Mother's Day and Father's Day.

However, that was likely not the kind of family you lived in. The closest your family came to the Huxtables was Bill Cosby's one unfortunate line to his son: "I brought you into this world—and I can take you out of it!" That was the reality of your family's relationships—threats of violence and annihilation, the destruction in word and deed of all that you held dear, personally and in your family. You lived in constant fear for your well-being and the survival of your family. Your welfare and your life were entirely dependent on the whim of a parent who had brought you into the world. Holiness was not what you felt in your family but rather terror and shame and degradation. Mother's and Father's Day sermons did not describe anything to which you could relate. Such sermons were another source of shame—you knew you did not belong in this community. Your family did not resemble what was being described as the standard—you did not measure up. And it was probably your fault because every other problem in your family was your fault. You were the unholy cause of all the problems in your family.

Were you really the cause of all those problems? Were you really so bad that you deserved those beatings? Did your spilled milk or smart remark or late arrival home really merit those bruises that you had to hide in school? Were you really being seductive when you climbed into your father's waiting lap? What about the times he came to your room uninvited? And if you are a wife who has been beaten and terrorized by her husband, was the late dinner or the amount of makeup you wore to the party really justification for the beatings you received? Was all that just proper discipline and the way one keeps children and wives in line?

The reality is that many families in our society, and even in our churches, are a far cry from anything exemplifying the sanctity of marriage and sacredness of the family. Many families, even among those that regularly attend church and synagogue, are places of shame and fear, of pain and humiliation, of distrust and anxiety rather than sources of holiness and faithfulness and hope. The reality is that many religious families do not live up to the ideals they profess or the images they project to the world around

them. They are physically, psychologically, and spiritually destructive to the very persons they are formed to nurture and foster
in the knowledge and love of God.

The question remains: Was your family abusive? Were you—a
member of a good religious family—a victim of abuse? Were you
abused if you were spanked? Or was it abuse only if you required
hospitalization? Is every wife who is ever pushed or slapped a
battered woman?

There is clearly an extensive continuum and many variations
when one talks about violence in a family. There are few precise
measures to determine when the discipline of a child, whether
physical or verbal, becomes abusive, or to ascertain when a bitter
disagreement between spouses becomes excessive. Yet we must
be careful not to justify corporal punishment and hurtful verbal
exchanges simply because they happen in the family.

A double standard exists when our society distinguishes between violence within families and that between acquaintances
and even strangers in the broader society. A push or a shove or a
slap of a colleague could well result in instant lawsuit or criminal
charges. Yet a similar incident in a family, even between adults, is
considered a family matter and should not be interfered with. All
too often such behavior, particularly on the part of a husband, is
considered an acceptable way to keep "his woman" in line. It is
interesting to note that one of the first legislative acts in the
United States to control wife battering instituted the "rule of
thumb". According to this law a husband was allowed to beat his
wife as long as he did not use a stick bigger around than the size
of his thumb. This was considered a step forward in social
legislation! It afforded some protection to the wife. It provided
some level of damage control.

Fortunately, it is becoming increasingly true that such approaches to child rearing and family life are no longer acceptable.
Through psychology we have gained important insights into the
complex processes involved in the development of a healthy
personality. As these processes become clearer, we are learning
how profound an impact the treatment accorded children has on
their later lives. We are learning that violence between intimates
has emotional and spiritual ramifications that far exceed the
obvious physical ones. We are beginning to look carefully at what

we consider acceptable. We are starting to develop guidelines for how we treat our children that are clearer, more specific, and less violent. We are discovering that there are alternative, nonviolent methods of discipline, training, and conflict resolution that are definitely less harmful and surprisingly more effective.

Without obsessively branding every form of discipline as criminal or arguing about the fine points of what constitutes abuse, our purpose here is to ask, What was harmful? What created distortions in your life? What was so painful? The critical question is: Did it have a negative effect on personal growth and development? Such a criterion may not be adequate for prosecuting a person for child abuse or wife battering, but that is not our concern. The issue in this book is what harmful things happened that you need to overcome and heal. Much abuse perhaps cannot be proven in a court of law and may be beyond the legal statute of limitations, but it is still personally and spiritually a devastating reality in your life.

Although all forms of abuse are damaging, it is important to recognize there are differences. Each form creates different personality and behavior dynamics. Each has different effects on later life and different impacts on the physical and emotional development of the persons experiencing them. The relationship between abuser and victim can affect the long-range impact of the violence. The age at which the abuse occurred will determine the effects on the developmental processes of a child. The forms of assistance and support available to a child can influence the range, depth, and longevity of the abuse's impact on later life.

All of those factors can magnify or mitigate the psychological and spiritual damage inflicted. Examining all such factors would take volumes. The kinds of abuse that we will examine here are physical, sexual, verbal, psychological, spiritual, and emotional. We will also examine the impact of what might be called a more passive form of abuse, neglect.

Not all violence in a family is directed toward children. There is also violence between the adult members of the family. The most common forms are the battering of wives and of elders. Sibling violence is also prevalent and is, in fact, the "most common form of family violence" (Gelles and Cornell 1985, 85). We will also consider these.

Physical Abuse

Physical abuse involves the striking of a child by parents or care-givers. It ranges from a mild swat on the behind, intended to get the child's attention, through a much more violent swat that leaves a bruise, to beatings that break bones and endanger life. The gentle swat may startle more than harm and may have little long-range impact beyond gaining the attention that was sought. Bruises and broken bones clearly are harmful. However, we need to ask, Is that really the extent of the damage?

At a campus ministry conference, Doris Bettes read a moving short story that raises just this question. The story is about an infant in a small, southern town who is severely beaten by her father, who also kills her mother. The father is imprisoned and another family takes the baby girl as their own daughter. No one in the town tells her about her real father and what he did, but everyone knows that someday he will return. Even though her bruises and broken bones have healed and the little girl was too young to remember what happened to her, everyone in town wonders, "Do the bones remember?" Do other effects remain after the bones have mended?

At one level this question is difficult, even impossible, to answer. The abuse occurred early in the child's life when she was preverbal; she did not have the cognitive experiences and skills to identify, much less articulate, what happened to her. The breaks in bones may heal and even become stronger at the point of the break; but the crushing of the spirit that accompanied the physical damage heals neither so easily nor so well—even in an infant. Negative messages attached to the beatings, whether expressly stated or only intuitively felt, remain to undermine a person's self-esteem and ability to trust another human being. When this abuse happens early in a child's life, he or she is unable to articulate what happened or what he or she feels. But when such persons try to focus on their early life, they are overwhelmed by a deep sense of dread and terror. They have what some psychologists call "body memories." This kind of harm, because of its difficult to define nature, often takes a long time to sort out, accept, and understand. It is a process that is extremely painful.

It was the recognition by emergency room doctors that the bones of some young children had been broken repeatedly and in unusual ways that led to the present awareness of the extensiveness of child abuse in our society. Alert doctors began to realize that certain childhood injuries were occurring in unusual forms and in patterns that were too consistent to be accidental. The resultant investigations by child welfare agencies revealed the frightening pervasiveness of the violence being done to children.

Physical abuse of this kind is the easiest to identify. It is also the most commonly reported because broken bones and multiple bruises are easy to verify. However, not all physical abuse results in a visit to an emergency room and bones do not have to be broken to have something to remember. You may have been slapped, punched, and even thrown across the room without an injury necessitating medical treatment. But you were certainly harmed, your physical well-being damaged, and your sense of security threatened, not only for that moment but for the foreseeable future. Even when you were too young to articulate it, the question remained, "When will this happen again? What did I do to deserve it? What must I do to avoid it in the future?"

To consider the impact of this treatment on your emotional development you need only realize that in that situation your physiological need for safety was not being met. Safety is identified by Abraham Maslow as the second in his hierarchy of needs, emerging as soon as the need for food is satisfied. Maslow maintains that satisfactory fulfillment of this need is essential before a person can move on to fill other needs and develop other aspects of one's personality. If one lives in constant fear for one's safety, little energy or attention can be directed to the pursuit of higher, more fulfilling goals of belonging, love, and self-esteem (1987, 15–23). One's personality development is thereby stunted. Is it surprising that you sometimes feel stuck in your process of personal and spiritual growth and development? There's good reason! But you need not be forever stuck. You can break free, you can grow personally and achieve a deep spirituality. Remembering is the first step, but unfortunately there are still several other forms of abuse to be considered before we can move on.

Sexual Abuse

Sexual contact between a child and another person who has some form of authority over that child is sexual abuse. Most commonly that person is a parent, but it may also be an older sibling, an uncle or aunt, a stepfather or mother, a grandparent or a baby-sitter or a trusted neighbor. The abuser may be of the same or different sex as the child. The abuse may take the form of touching, fondling, or sexual intercourse. It may involve suggestive remarks, leering, or inappropriate nudity. The critical issue is that some form of sexual activity is imposed on a subordinate by one with whom such conduct is inappropriate because of age difference or family relationship. That person is responsible for the care and protection of the child.

This sexual imposition may or may not involve physical violence. If the physical act is violently forced upon the child, he or she experiences the dual abuse of physical pain and sexual exploitation. The child now feels not only physically attacked but violated in the most intimate way possible. The confusion that ensues is doubly agonizing: "Maybe some reason can be found to explain why my father hits me—I failed to clean my room or I said something wrong. But why is my father doing this shameful thing to me? What did I do to deserve this? What kind of terrible person must I be?"

Often the trusted authority figure does not force the child into sexual activity. He cajoles, tricks, or "kindly" manipulates the child into a sexual relationship. Rewards of toys, money, or clothes are offered. The child is convinced that such contact is okay. It is "what you do to be nice to your uncle."

However, if this happened to you, you know that soon another message is added: "This is just something between us. This is not something we tell anyone else. It is just our little secret." Although the act was supposedly good before it happened, it is clearly wrong after the fact. Even before you were old enough to explain why, you knew that something was wrong. You were made to realize that it involved something that should not be told to others. It was something to hide and to be ashamed of.

When you grew older and learned the social taboos associated with such actions, your sense of shame and need for secrecy increased. A sense of horror and revulsion developed. You felt betrayed and psychologically as well as physically violated. The special trust that previously existed between you and your parent or care-giver had been destroyed.

Sexual abuse may also be committed by a total stranger. As

harmful as that may be (and it is!), the impact is not the same. Although the child's body is equally violated, the sense of betrayal is not as great. The level of social shame and disgrace is less. Such a sexual imposition has not entailed the same breaking of trust and the same failure of care and protection as there would be if the perpetrator had been a supposedly loving member of the family.

The betrayal of a loving and protecting relationship is an important aspect of the dynamic involved in sexual abuse. Not only does the sexual abuse experienced destroy the caring and protective relationship that had existed, it also destroys the whole system of care and protection believed to exist within a family. As a victim of such abuse you could not help but wonder, even subconsciously, why other members of your family did not interfere: "Even if my father was doing such an evil thing, why didn't my mother stop it? I can't believe she didn't suspect. Didn't she care enough about me to stop it? Was I so evil? Didn't she even think I was worth the effort?" Subconsciously you internalized a whole series of negative messages.

As a victim of sexual abuse you also faced other internal conflicts. As you became more and more horrified and disgusted by what was done to you and by the manner in which your natural childhood desire to please and be affectionate and caring was being exploited and manipulated, you may have started to ask, "Why didn't I stop it? Why didn't I tell someone?" You probably began to blame yourself for not stopping the relationship, for not telling someone. Thus mired in shame and guilt, you were unable to acknowledge what you knew in your heart, that as a child you did not have the physical or emotional strength to stop the abuse and that there really was no one to tell. The other members of the family were willing to ignore what was happening or they were not psychologically strong enough or emotionally independent enough to force the abuser to stop. The reality was that you had no way to stop the abuse and no one to turn to for help.

If the sexual abuse was not violent—and sometimes even when it was—you may have been aware that you experienced pleasure from the sex act. This may further horrify, disgust, and shame you: "How could I enjoy something so revolting? What must be wrong with me if I could take pleasure from this?" Once again your quagmire of guilt and shame wipes out the rational recognition that such sensations are involuntary physiological responses and are something over which you did not have control.

It should be evident that sexual abuse not only violates a child's rights to bodily integrity but also inflicts severe mental and emotional anguish. Whether or not your sexual abuse was accompanied by violence, the message imparted was that you were not an important person with valued rights. You learned that you were not worth protecting and were only an instrument for another person's pleasure. You were inculcated with an intense sense of degradation and depravity as well as deep feelings of disgust for—and yet preoccupation with—sex. You were subjected to profoundly confusing messages about sexuality and the role of sex as an appropriate expression of affection.

Verbal Abuse

Physical and sexual abuse are the most commonly identified forms of abuse. They constitute the cases most frequently reported to and investigated by child welfare agencies. Their immediate effects can be documented and judged. However, those who have been abused know only too well that with both these forms of abuse the immediate physical effects are only part of the damage done. Many other harmful and damaging messages are also transmitted; they are often more lasting than the physical pain.

However, these same messages can often be transmitted without ever a hand touching you. Such is the stuff of verbal abuse. Verbal abuse is the regular and consistent verbal degradation and belittling of a child by an authority figure responsible for the care and development of that child. It can involve explicit insults, name calling, and put-downs. It can entail rejection or denial of successes and accomplishments.

Such abuse cannot be measured or documented; it is not the matter for court cases and newspaper stories, but it is just as devastating. Those who experienced verbal abuse in their homes may want to revise the childhood retort used with such comfort during name-calling battles, "Sticks and stones may break my bones, but words will never hurt me." The saying may still be true when dealing with words coming from a childhood antagonist, but when the words come from the lips of parents, from the mother who was supposed to love, "the words can forever hurt." In this context the words of Psalm 55 may have special meaning:

> It is not enemies who taunt me—
> I could bear that;
> It is not adversaries who deal insolently with me—
> I could hide from them.
> But it is you, my equal,
> my companion, my familiar friend.
>
> (vs. 12–13)

As the psalmist poignantly tells us, messages from such sources strike us deeply. They remain long after any physical bruises have healed. These messages create deep wounds that become infected with malicious cancers of self-doubt, fear, insecurity, and a profound sense of helplessness and worthlessness. Such wounds do not heal naturally and simply over time. They must be cut open, examined, and excised by a long and often painful process of identifying, probing, and confronting the multitude of negative messages internalized over the years. Even after such a process, these wounds will not heal without ample doses of the ointment of loving care and support. Much hurt remains to be healed.

Psychological Abuse

It should be clear by now that all abuse has psychological dimensions. These dimensions are the most long-lasting and the most difficult of all the effects of abuse to identify and to treat. However, abuse may also be primarily and even exclusively psychological. It may even have involved little or no physical contact and may not have been physically violent. Such abuse may be inflicted without words and without any blows that could leave visible marks. Its wounds are on the spirit and psyche. Psychological abuse consists of the regular and consistent efforts of a care-giver to denigrate, control, or intimidate a child by fear, mocking, isolation, or spoken and unspoken threats.

Garbarino and Gilliam identify four aspects of psychological abuse:

1. Punishing positive, operant behaviors such as smiling mobility, exploration, vocalization, and manipulation of objects. . . .

2. Discouraging caregiver-infant attachment. . . . Such attachment is critical for child development and its disruption can have profound effects.
3. Punishing self-esteem. . . . To discourage self-esteem attacks a fundamental component of a person's development.
4. Punishing interpersonal skills necessary for adequate performance in nonfamilial contexts such as schools and peer groups . . . (1980, 74–75).

As a child you were by nature dependent. In order to survive and thrive, you needed regular care and nurture as well as adequate food, clothing, and shelter. Your mind and body as well as your character and personality were in the process of formation. You were highly susceptible to forces around you. You knew that you were dependent and had few, if any, resources outside your family. So if as a child you were paraded naked before snickering visitors, were not allowed to play with other children, were locked in closets for long periods of time, were forced to watch pets or possessions being destroyed, or were told that you might be given or sold to an unsavory relative or neighbor, you had little or no choice but to submit to the ridicule and intimidation. You had few alternatives but to live in constant dread and accept such conditions as a "normal" way of life. Although no blow may ever have been inflicted, you lived in fear that you might be the next victim of the same violence that destroyed your beloved pet. Even though no specific insult was uttered, your opportunities for personal development were severely hampered.

Sometimes such intimidation was experienced when you watched one of your parents beat the other. You wondered, "Will I be the next object of this anger? What will become of me if he kills her? What will happen to me if they separate? Is all of this fighting my fault? What did I do wrong?" Such thoughts may or may not have been the result of specific remarks by either parent, but the emotional distress was nonetheless real. The pain of the moment was no less intense and the psychological wounds were no less deep. The same negative messages were as deeply imbedded in your mind and heart as if they had been accompanied by violence. These messages continue into your adulthood to taint your view of yourself and the people around you. Even now you may find it difficult to feel good about yourself or trust others.

Spiritual Abuse

Spiritual abuse is not a form of family violence commonly identified by those who work in the field of domestic violence. However, in workshops on spirituality for survivors, survivors themselves have raised it as a way in which they experienced abuse. One woman referred to herself as a "recovering Roman Catholic." There are probably lots of recovering Baptists and Lutherans and Episcopalians as well.

In one sense spiritual abuse is a variation on verbal and psychological abuse; it uses the same methods and invokes similar dynamics, but it adds another dimension. Spiritual abuse consists of verbal attacks and put-downs or efforts to intimidate and control using religious language, beliefs, and rituals as the primary methodology.

Spiritual abuse has many forms. In its most extreme form, it is seen in satanic rituals. Ritual abuse incorporates all forms of abuse—physical, sexual, psychological—into a (pseudo) worship context, ascribing religious images and motivations to the violations being inflicted.

In its more subtle forms spiritual abuse employs religious categories, teachings, and standards to control or demean a person and invokes predictions of divine punishment if the abuser's "spiritual expectations" are not fulfilled: "You are an evil and wicked child! God will punish you! You will burn in hell!"

Such admonitions are used by parents, but they are also employed by religious leaders for adults as well as children. Johnson and VanVonderen focus their examination of spiritual abuse on "a leader [who] uses his or her *spiritual position* to control or dominate another person." This can involve *"the mistreatment of a person who is in need of help, support or greater spiritual empowerment, with the result of weakening, undermining or decreasing that person's spiritual empowerment"* (1991, 20, emphasis theirs). Spiritual abuse can also take the form of clergy exploitation of parishioners in addition to the failure to provide appropriate spiritual care. Such abuse involves not only the distortion of religious concepts but also the destructive use of religious authority.

Spiritual abuse may involve using religious justifications for abusive behavior: "Spare the rod and spoil the child" is a favorite adage of violent parents. It is invoked as a biblical admonition even though it is not actually found in the scriptures (see Appendix A, "Religious Messages That Destroy Spirituality"). Children, as they are being beaten, are often told to "honor thy Father and thy Mother." Sometimes they are even told, "You should let Daddy touch you this way because you should honor your father." All too often women are told that their failure to be "subject to their husbands" is the reason they are being beaten. Such messages can be voiced by abusive husbands, but they are also often reinforced by religious advisors.

Such uses of religious concepts and authority create profound confusion in the minds of the victims. How can they challenge what is being done to them? Even though what is being done to them feels wrong, they are being told it is right. These religious messages also create distorted images of God and religion that undermine and block spiritual avenues for healing. The most insidious aspect of spiritual abuse is that it adds another level of power and authority to the negative messages rampant in the other forms of abuse. To challenge and change these destructive "tapes," the power of divine judgement as well as human authority must be confronted. This is an overwhelming task for anyone brought up in an authoritative or fundamentalist tradition. Those who deal with survivors of satanic abuse speak with awe and even a little fear of the controlling power of that form of abuse.

Spiritual abuse is not a new phenomenon in religious circles. The Hebrew prophets were frequently challenging the way religious teachings and authority were being used. Jeremiah lamented that "scoundrels are found among my people; . . . Like fowlers they set a trap; they catch human beings" (5:26). Ezekiel decried religious leaders who "have devoured human lives" (Ezek. 22:25). Jesus challenged those who "tie up heavy burdens, hard to bear, and lay them on the shoulders of others; but they themselves are unwilling to lift a finger to move them" (Matt. 23:4). Jesus minced no words about religious authorities who misused their message and their power. He called them "ravenous wolves" (Matt. 7:15) and a "brood of vipers" (Matt. 12:34). Strong language about a serious problem.

Neglect

The forms of abuse discussed thus far are all active in their expression, no matter how subtly they may be executed. They all involve the utterance of a word or the commission of a deed of a hurtful nature. On the other hand, neglect is indirect. The abuse is not inflicted by words or deeds but rather is imparted by means of words not spoken and deeds not performed. A child is harmed because caring words are never spoken, because food, clothing, and shelter are not provided, because signs of affection are never offered. Neglect is the failure of care-givers to provide for the physical and health needs of a child under their care or to meet the child's emotional, affection, or support needs.

Physical neglect may be discovered in a hospital emergency room when children are brought in suffering from malnutrition or diseases resulting from unsanitary living conditions. Simple childhood diseases may have been allowed to progress to dangerous levels. Neglect may be identified when a neighbor discovers that a small child has been left alone for long periods of time, left to fend for itself at an age when it does not have the capacity to provide for its own well-being or to protect itself from harm. When this happens, child welfare agencies are called to investigate. If the situation appears chronic, the agency may instruct parents on proper care for the child. If such interventions do not solve the problem, the agency may remove the child from the home.

Despite the good intentions involved in such an action, there are few if any truly good ways to remove a child from an abusive setting. Despite the violence or neglect that may have occurred, this was the home with which you were familiar and the relationship patterns you recognized. The institution or foster home in which you may have been placed was an unknown environment and may have also had abusive elements. Child protection workers are progressively learning more about recognizing abusive settings and the most helpful ways to intervene. They still have much to learn. Survivors such as yourself have much to teach a system that has the welfare of children as its primary interest but is sometimes forced to choose between an undesirable but less harmful situation.

Neglect may also take a purely emotional form when parents fail to provide adequate affection for their children. Emotional neglect is only rarely seen in medical facilities. Such neglect is discovered in a medical setting when an infant is brought in who is failing to grow and develop. This "failure to thrive" is a medical diagnosis often associated with the fact that a child has not received adequate human contact. The infant does have enough food but has not been held, hugged, or cuddled enough to fulfill its emotional needs. The child's body fails to grow because it is starved for human affection. No matter how much food is available the child is too emotionally and physically listless to take advantage of it. Such a child can, in fact, die from a lack of adequate human affection. The most effective form of medical treatment for such a child is simply that she or he be held and hugged while being fed.

Emotional neglect in later years may not have dramatic physical consequences but may create frustration and depression. As neglected children grow older they learn to adapt to lack of physical contact. If you were neglected you expected that your mother would not touch you, would seldom speak to you, and would ignore you for long periods of time. Any other type of behavior would have been a surprise and even disconcerting. You learned to expect your mother's silence as a form of violence. You may have accommodated to your lack of emotional nurturing by developing a cold and distant and even hostile demeanor as you "learned" that the world was a cold, distant, and hostile place.

Emotional neglect often results from the parents' inability to provide for their own needs, let alone those of a child. The parent is sick or depressed and is unable to function in a caring or supportive way. If this was the nature of your family, you were forced to take care of yourself in ways far beyond the skills appropriate to your age. As a five-year-old you may have cared for younger siblings. As a seven-year-old you cooked for a family of six. As a teen you were responsible for filling out Aid for Dependent Children forms and negotiating with welfare agencies. Such responsibilities drained you. Even if you "performed your tasks well," the toll taken on your emotional development was devastating. The drain on your emotional reservoir was enormous. You probably felt empty and barren. Such is the natural response to such unnatural and overwhelming responsibilities.

In your family you were, in effect, taking over the roles of your parents. You ended up fulfilling many of the care-giver roles that were more appropriately the responsibilities of your parents. Often the roles that you performed were not merely those of the physical care-giver. You also became responsible for the emotional care and nurturing of your parents. Because mother was "feeling poorly," you had to soothe and care for her. Because Daddy was drunk so often that he could not be a supportive partner to his wife, you had to take on the role of a mature companion, and perhaps even of sexual partner. For you your family was not a place "for cooperative mutual support and affection but for exploitation and the satisfaction of neurotic needs" (Justice and Justice 1976, 70). In your family your needs were seldom met. You were left emotionally starved.

Your hunger for emotional support may be exemplified by a poignant event that occurred during one meeting of a Grown-Up Abused Children group. The group had been meeting for several weeks when a young woman arrived clutching a copy of a magazine article in her hand. She was visibly anxious throughout the meeting but refused to share the source of her anxiety. Finally, as the meeting neared its end, she gathered her courage and spoke in a voice that was as demanding as it was anxious, "This article says that everyone needs six hugs a day for their mental health. And I want mine! I figure that because of my family life I'm thousands of hugs behind. I want a hug from everyone here before we leave today!" The group members were startled but responsive. They all both feared and hungered for such human contact. For some, human touching was unknown; for others, it had only been a source of pain. All were anxious to learn what gentle, caring contact could be like in their lives. Everyone exchanged hugs at the end of that meeting. Someone suggested we do it again at the next meeting. It became the ritual conclusion for every session. In some fashion, that same question comes up in most other groups and some method for exchanging hugs is devised. The group provides the supportive, caring environment never available in the members' families. The group becomes one of the major sources of emotional nurture.

Other Forms of Family Violence

Violence between parents and children is not the only form that occurs in our society. Although the methods of violence are the same—physical, sexual, verbal, psychological, spiritual, and neglect—when it occurs between different parties in the family, different dynamics come into play. We will now consider the violence between some of those parties and the special ways they are destructive to the family and its members as well as the unique forms of pain that must be acknowledged and confronted if hope is to emerge.

Battering

The other form of family violence most well known in our society is that occurring between adult partners in a relationship. Although the most common form is that of husbands battering their wives, women are also known to have struck and harmed their husbands. However, the violence initiated by husbands is usually more serious because men are generally larger and stronger than women and thus able to do more harm. Men also seem to be physically more able and culturally more inclined to resort to violence. In Western society men generally also possess the economic and social power that allows them to escape the consequences of their actions. If men are the recipients of the violence, they possess economic and social options for escape unavailable to women. Therefore, the psychological impact of violence on women by their spouses is more devastating than for men. The reported cases of battered husbands are also minuscule compared to those of battered wives. This is not to imply that the battering of husbands is not devastating to those who are abused. It is only to say that the implications are different because the social realities of men and women are different.

At first glance, the dynamics of adults attacking one another would seem to be significantly different from those involved when adults abuse children. In the first place, a different relationship exists. The level of dependency and helplessness on the part of a battered wife is not nearly as extensive as that of a minor. A wife supposedly has more options and more avenues of escape. She should be able to get out of the situation.

However, if you have been in this situation, you know that those options and avenues exist only in theory. When you were in the abusive relationship, you know you felt as dependent and helpless as any child when it came to trying to separate from your battering husband. The battering you received made you feel too worthless, frightened, and ineffective to make any substantial move away from your violent situation. You may have been convinced that your battering was a punishment you deserved or the way you were to be subject to your husband or that it was something you had to endure to preserve the sanctity of your marriage. You may have been economically dependent on your abuser, and if you had children, you had financial and housing needs that could not be easily met. You believed, and often rightly so, that you had no one to turn to for help and no way to break the cycle. You were as emotionally locked into the situation as a child who is physically dependent upon his or her family. Your batterer skillfully made you feel powerless and removed whatever options may have existed for you.

Recall what was previously said about the psychological abuse inflicted on children when parents attack one another. Fear and anxiety pervade their lives and color their images and expectations of family life, marriage, and the nature of relations between men and women. Thus, even though they never experience a single blow they are still victimized in that family. This is a critical reality for a child in a home where battering is occurring.

Sibling Abuse

Violence between siblings is extremely common and widely accepted as "part of growing up." It is thought by many to be a normal part of a child's learning process. Through fights with brothers and sisters one "learns to take it," learns how to survive in a competitive world. Such violence is so commonly accepted that researchers find it difficult to study. Parents do not consider what their children are doing uncommon enough to report.

Sibling violence varies considerably depending on the age and sex of the children and also on variations in age and sex between the children involved. If, for example, you were abused by a brother or sister who was considerably older, the physical or sexual abuse can have impacts similar to those experienced if a parent had been the offender. In addition, you may rightly wonder why your parents did not protect you and you may develop considerable anger about their failure to protect.

Even if you and your brothers and sisters were close in age, acceptance of sibling violence taught you that violence is an approved way to solve problems. If, as often happens, you were the family scapegoat, you learned messages of inferiority and came to believe that your parents did not care for you. All such messages had negative impacts on a your development similar to those already discussed.

Elder Abuse

Although abuse toward adults can take many forms, such as parents abusing their adult children or adolescent and adult children beating their parents, the abuse of elderly persons is particularly devastating because of their especially vulnerable position. This matter demands increasing consideration as the demographics of our society change.

Abuse of the elderly can take many of the same physical and mental forms as that inflicted on children. Because of their physical vulnerability, older adults can be subjected to much of the same injury, punishment, and intimidation as small children. It is also possible for them to be unreasonably confined or restricted in their contacts with others. Because older adults may have personal resources, such as money, home, or other property of value to others, they may be exploited by their children or care-givers. Their resources may be unlawfully or improperly appropriated by others. Such exploitation is condemned by elder-abuse laws.

Laws on elder abuse also point out that older adults can be neglected in much the same way small children can. Because of physical needs that may be the result of infirmity, the failure to provide certain goods and services—such as medication, house-keeping and personal care assistance—can produce physical harm, mental anguish, or even mental illness.

If you are an older person who is being or has been abused, you are often as limited in your options as a child. You may be vulnerable and dependent because of illnesses or lack of re-sources. Often you are more cut off from society than are children. Your peers to whom you might turn for assistance may be as dependent as you or they may have died. As an older adult you have no social institution such as a school or job to which you are expected to relate and from which you might expect assis-tance. To seek assistance you must admit that you raised a child who is capable of such behavior. If you seek relief, you are often branded as a "nasty, unappreciative, old ———." With such forces at work, it is small wonder that abused older persons often report many of the same problems as grown-up abused children—namely, mistrust, low self-esteem, depression, and help-lessness. Such emotions are the sources of lost hope, the stuff of crushed dreams. They are personal feelings that stunt and distort spirituality.

We have considered the origins of your pain. Now we must consider the forms presently taken by that pain; we need to understand how the negative images from your past that infect your dreams affect your ability to dream great dreams for your future.

3 | Recovering Crushed Dreams

Families are the training grounds for society's children, the seedbeds of their spirituality. Families form their visions and generate or destroy their dreams. Child psychologists maintain that the first four years of life are the most significant for the character formation of children. What happens in the family is the single most important determinant of what children do and become in later life, and how they view their possibilities for growth. In families, basic human needs are met. Families are the places in which the primary developmental crises that shape personalities are to be resolved. What happens when these needs are not met, when these crises go unresolved, or are resolved in negative or harmful ways?

Volumes of studies tell us that many families are not healthy or even safe places for children to grow up. In fact, because of their families, many children do not live long enough to reach adulthood. The number one cause of death for children under age five is violence in their families.

Fortunately, most abused children are not killed. You survived to become an adult. Most women battered in their homes also survive to form other relationships. But even if you were fortunate enough to survive, what is your life like? What problems and anxieties do you face? What are your needs and what is the status of your dreams?

When Elizabeth Carmichael and I formed the first Grown-Up Abused Children group, we were only vaguely aware that the students with whom we had talked had similar problems. We knew that they all felt isolated, but we did not understand the exact nature of the problems they had experienced. Neither did we understand the connections between their present problems and their past abuse. All we knew was that they felt isolated and alone, and that they had been abused. Was a support group a good treatment method? We were only guessing. What dynamics would develop when we brought together a group of students with similar family backgrounds? We really did not know.

More inclined to foolishness than bravery and guided more by the Spirit than our combined knowledge of counseling and psychology, we simply jumped into the task. Generally speaking, the first group went well. Sometimes it foundered, other times the members blossomed through new insights and growth, but always the group continued to meet. In fact, we had to beg them to take a break. Frequently, we as leaders met together to discuss what was happening and to try to analyze why. We gradually became clearer and more adept at what we were doing. Our confidence in what we were doing and how we should do it increased.

Frequently, Elizabeth and I—and later other coleaders—met together to analyze what we saw happening. We identified patterns within the problems we were encountering. We noted connections between behaviors and relationships between present problems and past experiences. We identified major problem areas. When the Grown-Up Abused Children program began to expand in Cleveland and new leaders needed to be trained, my coleader at the time, Laura (Wilson) Webb, and I were forced to define and record our reflections. This resulted in our book, *Grown-Up Abused Children* (1985).

The problem areas we identified are not unique to survivors of abuse. They are, in fact, areas where all people who are struggling for optimum development of their personalities may have problems or may desire greater maturity. However, for you as a survivor the problems that arise are not merely a matter of a fuller life or of fine-tuning your sensitivities or of more fully developing your human potential. Your problems stem from the fact that because of your abuse experience you lack basic skills or have enormous gaps in your experience. You may also experience paralyzing fears related to the performance of basic and simple human relations tasks because of the violence that surrounded such activities in your home. The depth, intensity, and magnitude of the problems are also substantially different. Because you experienced many of these difficulties simultaneously, they constitute qualitatively different kinds of problems. The whole becomes greater than the sum of the parts.

The list of traits that we developed is not necessarily the only way to categorize the problems of grown-up abused children. Nor is it exclusively applicable to them. Ray E. Helfer describes the "World of Abnormal Rearing." This "W.A.R. Cycle" applies to many adults who missed out on certain aspects of their childhood (1984, 33–79). Lenore Walker identifies similar problems for battered women and their batterers (1979, 31, 36, 254). This list is, however, a good starting point for understanding some of the problems you may face, no matter what form of family violence you suffered.

We will examine factors generated by abuse that are common for all survivors: loss of trust, destruction of self-esteem, poor social skills, loss of power, fear of making decisions, and the repression of emotions. We will conclude with a discussion of the distortion of sexuality sometimes generated in sex abuse survivors.

Loss of Trust

Trust is a basic element in all human relationships. On it depends the ability to make friends, to form intimate relationships, and ultimately to establish lasting and fulfilling marriages. The ability to trust can be nurtured and strengthened by reflection, discussion, and structured experiences. But our fundamental orientation toward trust is formed by our basic life experiences. We learn to trust by having persons close to us treat us with respect, kindness, and consistency. We learn to trust by experiencing trustworthiness in others.

Erik Erikson (1963, 247–251) maintains that the developmental process that disposes a person toward trust or mistrust is the first psycho-social crisis in human experience. It occurs primarily between birth and the age of two. Much of it happens literally at our mother's knee.

But what happens when that mother is abusive? What happens when that mother is inconsistent? What does a child learn when one day he is hungry, he cries, and he is fed and yet the next day, when the same pain arises in his stomach and he makes the same response, that same mother beats him and no food is forthcoming? What will the "bones remember" when one day a child approaches her mother with open arms and is picked up, cuddled and caressed but the next day she is beaten and thrown across the room, and yet there is no apparent difference in the circumstances? This all too frequently is the experience of an abused child. Twenty percent of reported abuse cases involve children under the age of two. The lessons learned are all too clear, "I can't trust my mother. Since I can't trust my mother, who can I trust?"

You also learned another lesson. While this erratic process was going on, you—even as an infant—were trying to figure out, "What do I do to get a positive response? What will prompt my mother to give me food? What do I do to make sure she doesn't hit me?" Your answer was, "I do not know. Nothing seems to work consistently. I must be doing something different from one time to another, but I can't figure out what it is. There must be something wrong with my instincts. I can't trust myself." You learned, "I cannot trust other people and I cannot trust myself. They are untrustworthy and I am unreliable." All this you learned without the word "trust" ever being uttered.

Not all abuse starts in infancy. Initially parents may be caring and consistent, but later in childhood the relationship changes and becomes abusive. The reasons for this change can vary widely and are not the subject of this book. When the abusive and inconsistent behavior begins in later life, it is experienced at a more conscious level. Such experiences are more open to conscious reflection and redefinition than those remembered only "in the bones." However your internal conflict is still the same: "If I can't trust my parents who are supposed to love me, who can I trust? If I can't do anything right, I must be a worthless child."

Destruction of Self-Esteem

The fact that you as an abused child learned you could not trust your parents creates other problems. As Erikson points out, the ability to trust oneself and others "forms the basis in the child for a sense of identity which will later combine a sense of being 'all right,' of being oneself, and of becoming what other people trust one will become" (1963, 249). The ability to trust and to feel trustworthy had a profound effect on your childhood perceptions of yourself. If your parents did not care enough about you to provide consistent love and care, the message you internalized was that something was wrong with you. You were unlovable.

If learning you cannot trust your mother created problems, what happens when you realize that your mother also did not love you? If your mother did not love you, who will? This devastating question and its natural conclusions confront every grown-up abused child: "My parents did not love me. I must have been an awful child. Sure, sometimes they said they loved me, but they acted otherwise. I must be a terrible person."

Such conclusions are natural for a grown-up abused child. You were not simply punished when you broke a toy or teased your sister or hung around with the wrong crowd. You were not simply reprimanded when you did poorly in school or stayed out too late. You were also ridiculed when you did well in school and you were accused of being arrogant when you brought home awards. You were slapped around for no apparent reason and told repeatedly that you were stupid, ugly, unlovable, and a slut. The only consistent pattern in your life was abuse. There was no consistency to the reasons for which you were being punished.

In many cases you were not only punished for the mistakes you made or the rules you broke, you were also punished for who you were. Your parents did not distinguish between your childhood clumsiness or adolescent misdeeds and you as a person. You were perceived as inherently evil, not merely as someone who had done things that were wrong.

This failure to distinguish between you and your deeds was often coupled with your parents' unrealistic expectations for you. As pointed out in the discussion of neglect, many abused children are expected to fulfill roles in their families that are far beyond those appropriate to their age. This is not always a result of the parents' own inadequacies and inabilities to fulfill their own parental roles. It can also be the result of unrealistic expectations and confusion over roles in the family.

Parents often expect their children to meet the parents' physical and emotional needs. You were expected not only to clean your own room but the whole house. In addition, you were expected to be your parents' source of emotional support and the responsible decision maker in your family. When you failed in any of these adult tasks, you were branded as bad and evil and useless.

Years of being told that you are worthless and unlovable by the very people you expect to be the most understanding and accepting eventually takes its toll on your self-image. Years of childhood inability to fulfill adult responsibilities, which you were made to believe ought to be yours, convinced you that you are worthless.

If anyone outside your family treated you as someone worthwhile, that person must have been wrong or simply unaware of how bad you really are: "He doesn't know what my mother knows about me. If she knew me as well as my father does, she would not think so highly of me." You learned the negative messages well.

Poor Social Skills

If one does not trust oneself or other people or if one does not believe oneself to be worthwhile, that person is not going to reach out to others. There is nothing to be gained. Friendship is practically unknown. The survivor is convinced that even though people may be nice in the beginning, "they will soon turn against me. No one wants to be my friend anyway because I have nothing to offer."

You may recognize this approach to other people as one that is common for you. It is a natural consequence of an abusive background. Such an attitude works against the possibility that you as a survivor could learn common social skills. If you are afraid to interact with other people or are convinced that little or nothing can come from it, you are not going to make much effort to make friends or gain any of the social experiences associated with doing so.

This hesitancy to initiate social contacts with others creates a vicious cycle. Because it is difficult to talk to others, you do not know where to start when it comes to forming friendships. Your fear makes you appear aloof and standoffish. Therefore, others are reluctant to take the initiative. This lack of response on the part of others confirms your sense of worthlessness and makes taking the first steps toward friendships more difficult. As a result you have few friends.

In your mind this lack of friends confirms that you are a

failure, that you are worthless. You do not have friends because you are an uninteresting person. No one talks to you because you are not worth talking to. You are convinced that you are better off keeping to yourself. If someone does attempt to make friends with you, does try to get past the walls of aloofness and the barriers of isolation that you learned to erect in self-defense, that caring person may experience a wide variety of reactions.

Despite your desire that someone care for you, you may communicate distrust and even hostility to your prospective friend because you are sure that such caring behavior is not real and will not continue. Such suspicious responses are not the stuff of which strong friendships are made. Even the most caring and committed prospective friend will find his or her determination strained. Despite the best intentions of both of you, the friendship may be stifled.

Another response that you may unintentionally make is a grasping enthusiasm or suffocating attachment as you seek to fulfill all of your needs for affection in a single relationship. You may seek to gain all the acceptance you never found in your family. Such smothering attachment is also not the stuff on which friendships thrive. In either case you exhibit your lack of constructive social skills, which makes it difficult to create wholesome opportunities where such skills can be developed.

Your poor social skills are not merely the result of your lack of trust or feelings of poor self-worth. Your family also failed to provide the normal opportunities that most children have to learn the basic social skills of conversation and discussion. A common trait of abusive families is the lack of social interaction between members of the family. Typically, there is little or no general conversation and even less sharing of feelings and emotions. In fact, the latter are strongly discouraged and are often the occasion for violence. Such responses to discussion and sharing did not provide you with many occasions for developing the common social skills of conversation and communication of emotions.

Furthermore, children in abusive families are often hesitant to make friends with schoolmates. If you were able to disguise your "faults," which are so evident to your parents, you may have made friends with other children. But you knew you had to be careful not to become such good friends with your schoolmates that they might expect to visit your home. Such visits could have terrible consequences—your friends might visit your home and find out how your parents treat you and learn what a worthless person you really are. It was safer to limit your contacts with schoolmates than to take the chance that they will really find out what kind of person you are. Thus, your opportunities for learning the basic social skills that might have occurred through interactions outside the home were also limited because you were afraid to allow them to develop.

Another consequence of this hesitancy to develop friendships is that you never experienced other families up close. You never learned there are ways to relate to people, to confront disagreements, and to resolve conflicts that do not involve yelling, screaming, and fighting. You never learned to express your needs, to share confidences and to rely on friends for assistance. When a group member was once chided for not sharing some of her fears and asking for assistance, she responded sadly, "I didn't know I was allowed." She never learned that there can be people who do care and can help.

All of this increases the isolation you experienced and intensifies the feelings of mistrust and unworthiness that so color your life. When your life and relationships are controlled by such forces, the basic human tasks associated with forming and maintaining relationships become difficult and even excruciatingly painful.

Loss of Power

Because children are unable to determine what prompts caring behavior instead of assaults from their parents, they are unable to develop a sense of power or control over their lives. Human beings become empowered to give direction and purpose to their lives by learning to control the forces around them. This learning process begins with realizing one can get milk or a dry diaper by crying. It expands into learning to state one's needs, to communicate one's desires and even to express an opinion different from one's parents and having that opinion respected. This learning involves a process of trial and error in a supportive environment where successes are applauded and mistakes are occasions for learning.

This process does not happen in abusive families. Abusive parents are inconsistent in their treatment. Identical behaviors elicit reactions that range from caring to cruelty, from praise to punishment. Such inconsistent reactions cause confusion and bewilderment. Abused children rightly learn to feel that they can not have any effect over their own lives; they have no control over their environment. They are powerless.

As children grow older they go through many stages of development. Erikson (1963, 251–261) maintains that the critical psycho-social crises that occur after the development of trust focus on the development of autonomy, initiative, and industry. By resolving these crises children learn to take control over their lives, make decisions about their actions, and achieve a sense of accomplishment through their activities. Each stage requires that they learn new behaviors, take risks, and determine what achieves a desired end and what does not. In the process they experience power and achieve a sense of control over their lives.

In an abusive family this process is short-circuited. Your attempts at independent action were indiscriminately punished or praised. Your initiatives were at one time encouraged, at another mocked or attacked; your efforts to express yourself and to achieve self-determination were undermined and ridiculed. Instead of being encouraged and becoming empowered to control your life and destiny, you learned to be doubtful about your abilities, feel inferior to any task and guilty about your efforts. Because the responses by your parents did not follow a rational or consistent pattern, you could not determine the connections between your behaviors and the outcomes you experienced. Instead of gaining a sense of power, you learned helplessness. Therefore, the prospect of assuming control over your life becomes a task fraught with negative recollections. The possibility of undertaking new responsibilities in your job becomes excruciatingly painful and the act of making a decision becomes terrifying.

Fear of Making Decisions

Few people enjoy making decisions. We prefer to get what we want without having to make difficult choices. We would really rather cruise through life toward our goals on a smooth freeway without tempting exits and challenging detours. It would be nice if there were no hassle or anxiety. Unfortunately, life does not work that way. We do have to make decisions and decide between options that may be equally enticing. Life's a hassle, but somebody—everybody—has to do it.

Survivors know that the challenge of decision making poses more than an inconvenience and a few anxious moments. It is a task filled with doubt and guilt and a perceived inability to perform any task correctly. In addition to the emotional strain you experience, you simply may not know how to make decisions. The reasons for this can be summed up in five negatives: no models, no training, no opportunity, no evaluation, and no hope.

The first of these negatives arises from the fact that your own parents may not have known now to model decision making. They did not know how to analyze options or weigh consequences. Therefore, little effective decision making was done in your home. You had no opportunity to observe the process in action and learn from it. You had no models to follow.

You may not have had any training. Generally, your parents may have ignored you and let you survive by your own devices. As a child you received no guidance as you struggled through the progressively more difficult decisions involved in childhood and adolescence and, finally, adulthood. What you did learn about decision making, you learned by trial and error with no help in evaluating what you had done. You never received any assurance about what you were doing.

You may have had no opportunity to make decisions. Your parents did not allow it. They severely restricted the options available to you and told you precisely what to do. And you were expected to like it. Whether or not you liked alternatives imposed on you, you were being denied critical opportunities to learn how to make decisions for yourself.

Even if you were taught how to make decisions and allowed to make them, you may not have been provided any clear measure of your effectiveness. You may have been ignored to the extent that you would make decisions and no one would respond to what you had done. It was as if no decision had been made. No one noticed whether you had done a good job or a bad one. If the decision did have some negative consequences, no one was available to help you understand why and learn how to make better decisions in the future. You were never given tools to evaluate what you had done.

Your parents also may have changed the rules in the middle of the process; they may have changed the criteria for evaluation. You would be told to do one thing and then be punished because you did not do something else. You would be told that your parents did not care what you did and then you would be beaten for what you did do. You would be encouraged to choose whatever you wanted and then would be punished if the choice did not coincide with what was secretly desired by your parents. You were never given clear criteria with which to judge whether you had done a good job.

And finally, you may have been given no hope. Besides never receiving the guidance that could help you make successful decisions, often the matters about which you were to make decisions were far beyond the level of maturity you had attained. You were forced to make decisions that should have been the responsibility of the adult members of your family. Too many variables were involved for you realistically to be expected to make the correct decision. You were thrown into situations in which you were almost guaranteed to fail. The end result of all these negatives is that you did not learn the correct process for decision making and the task itself became fraught with memories of failure and pain.

As an adult survivor you may handle the anxiety related to decision making in two different ways. One is simply to do nothing. You may wait until the circumstances make the decision for you. Someone has said, "Not to decide is to decide." The quote is frequently used as a challenge to those who fail to take stands on important issues. However, for you the saying may be a source of consolation. It tells you that if you wait long enough the decision will be made for you and you will be relieved of the task and the anxiety attached to it.

The other way you may manage the anxiety related to decision making is to rush into a decision, grab the first option available, and run with it. When you act this way you do not have to bother to analyze alternatives and anguish over possible consequences: "Whatever decision I make will be wrong anyway, so why bother thinking about it?"

Neither method for decision making is a very effective way to manage one's life. The first response results in missed opportunities and a lack of control over your life. I see this frequently in students who wait so long to choose their classes that they are closed out of the ones they want or need. Then they become depressed because "nothing ever works out for me."

The second response results in poorly conceived life choices. You may see this response in your life as you seem to make the same mistake over and over again. This may be seen in the patterns of your intimate relationships. You repeatedly make poor choices in lovers and mates. You attach yourself to any person who responds positively without analyzing other aspects of the person's personality. You may frequently end up in relationships that are harmful and even abusive, and you do not understand what went wrong and why you made such a disastrous choice again.

Repression of Emotions

As I write about this topic, a lot of emotions well up. As you read this material you may also experience a lot of feelings—particularly old feelings about your abuse that you have long tried to block. As uncomfortable as those feelings may be, let yourself feel them. They are natural and healthy responses to what happened to you. If you admit and deal with them, they will not last forever.

One of the feelings you may be having is anger. It is certainly a common reaction for me when I hear or write about abuse. Anger, too, is a natural and healthy response—I will argue later that it is even a virtue. However, in your family you probably were not allowed to have such a feeling. You were told it was wrong and you learned that it was dangerous. In your family any sign of anger, especially when you were being beaten, would result in more abuse.

Such was your dilemma as an abused child. You had feelings, but you were forced to suppress them. You were not allowed to demonstrate your feelings and you often were severely punished if you did.

When you experienced frequent and harsh violence in your family, you quite naturally felt anger at your attacker. But frequently your attacker was your parent. Anger at one's parents is wrong. So says society: "Honor your father and your mother." So also said your parent, often with a few well-placed blows to reinforce the point.

You also knew that anger was a dangerous emotion. You had experienced its damaging results. If perchance you expressed the anger you felt, you often received violence in return. In your experience, anger and violence were integrally connected, one automatically led to the other. Seldom, if ever, did you see someone angry without some form of violence resulting. You do not want to be violent to others—you know how painful that can be. For you to avoid violence, you must avoid anger.

Therefore, you learned to deny any feeling of anger. To even acknowledge such a feeling was too dangerous. It opened up too many negative possibilities. You would certainly feel guilty; you might be punished, and you might do something harmful to someone else.

In the Grown-Up Abused Children groups many members insist that they do not and never have felt angry. They say this even as they grit their teeth and clench their fists. They learned that anger is something to be avoided at all costs. To avoid it they must deny its existence.

On the other hand, you may be able to admit some of your anger but not that toward your parents. That anger feels too wrong, too guilt-provoking to be admitted. Instead you may express your anger toward other persons and things. One woman began to recall her abusive background as she shouted angry slogans during a rally against the Vietnam War. She suddenly realized that much of the vehemence and rage behind her angry chants was really meant for her abusive parents.

Or you may realize that you acted in angry and even violent ways, but you experienced no emotion at the time. You may have been in situations that rightly provoked anger and you may have acted accordingly, but you did so with complete dispassion. You may have felt as if you were standing outside yourself watching another person perform acts that you recognized as angry and violent. The prospect of being angry was too threatening for you to allow yourself to be directly involved. You had to separate yourself from the person who was acting.

Much of such disassociation with one's own feelings is because of guilt you may experience over such feelings. Not only are you not supposed to be angry with your parents, but because you are such a worthless person, you also have no right to be angry. You would be doubly wrong to be angry at your parents.

This guilt associated with what most people would consider justifiable anger can create other problems. You may believe that because your anger is wrong you deserve to be punished. Any time you have even the slightest sensation of anger you feel you ought to be reprimanded. Because no one is available or willing to do so, you must do it to yourself. Many grown-up abused children report acts of self-mutilation or suicide attempts following episodes of feeling angry towards their parents. They feel obliged to hurt themselves as a form of punishment or as a way to make up for what they have felt.

The problem of identifying and expressing feelings may not only be associated with the "negative" feelings of anger and guilt, but also with positive emotions, such as joy and satisfaction. You may have been punished for your childhood exuberance. When you were excited and boisterous because something pleased you, you were slapped and told to shut up. When—as an older child—you expressed satisfaction at your accomplishments, you were ridiculed and beaten for being proud and arrogant. One woman reported that the worst beating of her life occurred after she rushed home from school to show off the new uniform she had received when she made the school band. Her father beat her so violently she had to flee the house to save herself.

Even normal responses to human situations were not acceptable. One group member told of the beating he received because his father found him crying over the death of his dog. "I'll give you something to really cry about," was the statement that preceded the beating.

The lessons learned from such experiences were that joy is dangerous, that pride and self-satisfaction are wrong, and that sadness is unacceptable. In short, all emotions should be suppressed; they certainly should not be expressed.

For many, one emotion was constant and easily identifiable—fear. You may yet be living in constant fear of being punished for anything and everything and of being rejected. You assess even your most minute actions for their potential for punishment—always expecting the worst. You may verge on the compulsive in your desire to please, always trying to determine what the people around you want, trying to anticipate their every desire. You believe you must determine this so you will not be rejected. Thus, your emotional touchstone is anxiety and fear as you attempt to identify and fill the emotional needs of others. At the same time, you ignore and deny your own needs and feelings. So much of your energy goes into dealing with the feelings of others you never learn to recognize your own. Over and over again we have asked members of our groups to tell us what they are feeling and have been met with blank stares. They do not even recognize the question as one appropriate to themselves.

Distorted Sexuality

Based on what we have said so far, it does not require great psychological sophistication to deduce that sexual abuse can create sexual problems. It is the most profound violation of a person's trust because sexual abuse, as we are considering it, constitutes sexual activity between a trusted family member or friend and someone (adult or child) who is nonconsenting. It thus destroys not only the person's bodily integrity but also her or his confidence in previously trusting relationships.

Survivors of sexual abuse do not have to be told that it is devastating because of the intimate nature of the violation and the secrecy and privacy involved. Sex is a private, intimate, and even a secret activity. When such acts are performed outside the "normal" parameters for such activity, the level of secrecy increases. In sexual abuse, the secrecy imposed reaches its zenith. As you know too well, to the natural privacy associated with sexual activity is added another message of secrecy and shame.

The perpetrator carefully constructed opportunities to be alone with you. He communicated the secrecy of the act. Sometimes this was done in a cajoling manner: "This is just between you and me. We won't be able to go to the park again, if you tell mother what we have done." At other times the message was imprinted in your mind by threats or beatings: "If you tell anyone, it will hurt others."

You may also have been aware that other members of your family were participants in the secrecy. Your mother quietly ignored the abuse or she made vicious or disparaging remarks about "Daddy's little darling," all the while offering no help or assistance. If the abuse occurred when you were older, you were made to feel responsible both by your abuser ("You are such an attractive young woman") and by others ("What did you do to make him do this?"). All of this enforced the need for secrecy and heightened your sense of guilt and shame associated with the sexual abuse.

If your sexual abuse was truly a secret in the family you may still wonder if it was because people chose to ignore anything related to sexual activity. Because it was too shameful to be considered, they preferred to look the other way. This reinforced your sense of shame and the need for silence.

If and when your sexual abuse did become public, the people who became involved may have responded with great horror and dismay. Authorities may have become involved and your family may have been broken up. Although such procedures were intended to protect you, they were nevertheless emotionally disruptive and may often have created further feelings of shame and guilt for you. Despite people's best intentions you were revictimized by the very processes set up to protect you. Such consequences are the result of evil actions in an imperfect world, which has not yet devised effective ways to heal the effects of evil.

If you were sexually abused, you may have learned either of two very different things. One thing you may have learned is that sex and any form of intimate physical contact is wrong, ugly, and threatening. For such women (and women are the most frequent victims), any form of intimate contact with a man creates tremendous anxiety. Even a friendly hug in passing can stir painful memories or precipitate great fear. The hug is perceived as a prelude to forced sexual intercourse. For such women the ritual hugs at our group sessions described above were threatening, but because they were performed in a safe and public environment, they produced meaningful learnings. As these women experienced caring contact without further sexual intimacy, they learned that such contacts can be separated from sexual activity and that they need not be occasions of great fear.

Those who have been able to establish loving and intimate relationships with men may, nevertheless, be frequently afflicted with recollections of sexual abuse episodes. Many survivors report flashbacks of abusive experiences in the midst of lovemaking. Such experiences place a cloud of apprehension over all future acts of intimacy and constitute a great deterrent to fulfilling sexual relationships.

Some may find the mere thought of sex with a man so

frightening or distasteful that they have opted for a lesbian relationship. I am not suggesting that sexual abuse experiences explain all homosexual orientation. It certainly may not be the sole reason for homosexual orientation among persons who did experience abuse. (Recent discoveries in biology and genetics indicate that homosexual orientation may be inherited.) However, it is easily understandable that some are too frightened by their past experiences to even consider the heterosexual alternative.

If you were sexually abused as a child, you may have learned something quite different. You may have learned to be flirtatious and even promiscuous in your relationships with men. You learned that the primary way to gain acceptance, approval, and affection from men is to offer yourself as an eager sex partner. Such sexual relations may or may not be satisfying, but that is not the issue. The purpose of such relationships is not to establish a meaningful relationship but to gain acceptance by whatever method works.

To date, little research has been done on boys who experienced sexual abuse. Although the incidents may in fact be less frequent than those of abuse of girls, there is increasing evidence that it happens more frequently than previously believed. The abuse may be either homosexual or heterosexual in nature. If the sexual abuse is mother to son there is evidence that the response will be similar to those described above for women who were abused by males: aversion or excessive acting out. In the latter case the men are often trying to reassert their manhood.

If the abuse is father to son, multiple confusions can be created. The grown-up abused child may experience an aversion to the behavior of the abusive father but have severe questions about his sexual identity and manhood. He may also question his ability to perform in a heterosexual manner. The young man clearly lacks models for normal sexual activity. When stricken with the typical confusion of puberty, such abuse survivors are practically guaranteed more than their fair quotient of adolescent anxieties.

The same anxiety about sexual identity may exist for women who were abused by their mothers. This is another area where little data has been gathered and little study has been done, but apprehension and confusion should not be unexpected.

Whatever the manner of response, as a sexual abuse survivor, you likely experience a high level of confusion about your sexual identity and about appropriate methods of sexual expression. This can create numerous problems for you as you seek to develop intimacy, establish loving relationships, and even select a mate with whom you might have a satisfying sexual relationship.

These issues are, of course, critical for all people. These are important life choices that affect people's prospects for happiness. It is, therefore, important that you as a survivor become increasingly conscious of the dynamics involved in the sexual abuse you may have experienced. Such information can help you more effectively care for yourself, heal your wounds, and develop meaningful and life-affirming relationships with others.

Such information is needed to understand better the effects of all forms of abuse. Child abuse has effects that extend beyond the immediate burns and bruises and belittling. It also conveyed negative messages. These messages continue throughout your life. These messages also tell you how to relate to others. Such methods may have been necessary and appropriate in an abusive family but are counterproductive in a nonabusive environment. However, you were not taught how to distinguish one situation from the other. Thus, you misapply the skills you learned so well. Immediate acts of abuse, as harmful as they were, imparted lessons that diminished your life. We will now seek to understand how these have affected your life, how what was done in your family betrayed your basic instincts for life and love, and how the training you received may continue to betray you.

4 | Challenging Lessons That Betray

Betrayal is the basic reality for a survivor of abuse. You were betrayed by the parent who abused you or by the parent who did not protect you. You were betrayed by your husband who said he loved you, yet beat you. You were betrayed by the family members who looked the other way when confronted with your bruises and scars. You may also have been betrayed later in your life by people who refused or were unable to understand the problems generated by your abuse and provide the support you needed. All such betrayal was and continues to be extremely painful.

To be told now that your own behaviors betray you, may make you feel like you are being blamed for your own pain—that you are your own abuser. It could be interpreted to mean that your dysfunctional behaviors caused your abuse, that your behavior as a child caused the violence you received. Nothing could be further from the truth. No childhood mischief justifies the violence that you and so many other abused children experienced. It is true that abused children are often rebellious, disobedient, and disruptive. Many teachers report that children from abusive homes exhibit severe discipline problems. The question is whether your rebellious behavior, if you were one of those children, was the reason you were abused or whether it was the result of your abuse. Was your behavior the result of activities you saw modeled in your home or was it your way of acting out feelings generated at home that you did not dare act upon there?

Certainly, the disruptive actions of children in school must be corrected and controlled. So also must the inappropriate and sometimes violent actions of adults be modified and corrected. However, one's approach to that correction will differ greatly depending on whether the actions are considered the result of inherent evil or the result of destructive forces imposed upon them by their families. Is the child just naturally bad or has he or she learned that disruptive behaviors are the only way to get attention at home, or that they are a way of acting out frustration with what is happening at home?

Our society might take a more sympathetic approach to treating disruptive and even violent persons if it had a better understanding of the extent to which the behaviors stem from their abusive experience and if it fully appreciated the aphorism, "Hurt people hurt people." The high number of prison inmates who were victims of child abuse tends to support this view. This is not to excuse their violent behavior, but it does suggest a different approach to treatment and rehabilitation.

However, even if you were disruptive as a child, you have likely learned to control your hostilities and frustrations well enough to function in polite society. You have found more creative ways to express your anger or you have gotten more effective in repressing it. However, angry outbursts are not the only disruptive acts possible. You can disrupt relationships by being too distant from other people or too clinging. You can alienate people by constantly testing their commitment to your relationship or by being overly sensitive to their every word and gesture. You can strain a relationship by the indirect and manipulative ways you try to maintain it. Such behavior can unintentionally betray your best intentions and ruin your best friendships.

You may not consider these behaviors inappropriate and may not even realize they are affecting your relationships. Therefore, you do not know there is something to change. The purpose of this chapter is to help you recognize some of the possible ways your actions may be betraying you so that you can achieve the insights necessary to modify the behavior that disrupts your relationships and your life. If you can understand the source of the behavior, you can change it to be more productive.

A brief story may illustrate this point. A few years ago an informal discussion at a clergy gathering turned to my work with grown-up abused children. The discussion continued for some time as pastors continued to probe me with questions about the nature of grown-up abused children. I was surprised with the intensity of their interest. When the group broke for dinner, one pastor identified the reason for his enthusiasm about the topic. He said, "You have just helped me understand a number of parishioners who have been driving me crazy. I knew they came from abusive backgrounds, but I did not understand what bearing that had on their present behavior." This chapter will share some of the content of that discussion and will highlight some of the behavior that may be common to you as a survivor that may not only be dysfunctional for you but aggravating for those who must live and work with you. Not all of this behavior is unique to survivors of abuse, but it is often more intense and pervasive with such persons.

Attachment to Approval

As we have noted, most survivors do not think very highly of themselves. You consider yourselves worthless and unlovable. This is the message you learned and internalized from your families. When you encounter someone who says something different, who affirms you as a person, and accepts you as someone of value, your reactions may be of two very different kinds: You may be pleasantly surprised and enthralled with such approval, or you may be suspicious and become anxious because the experience is so unfamiliar to you.

If you are one who is able to accept the positive messages, you may find the experience so exhilarating that you become strongly attached to the source of that approval. Finally, you have found someone or a group who accepts and appreciates you for what you are.

When you finally encounter a person or group who treats you as a person of value, you may see them as beacons of light in an otherwise dark world. The light of unconditional acceptance may entice you the way a light attracts moths. You may throw yourself at the light of approval randomly and compulsively without understanding why the light is so attractive or how it can be used to best advantage. You have found a place where you can receive the approval and affirmation you never received at home. In your hunger for affection you may become compulsively attached to such persons or groups. These persons may, without anyone understanding what is happening, become surrogate parents and families for you. Although such relationships can be beneficial, the parties involved need to understand the basis of the relationship. Otherwise, the extent and intensity of the attachment can become confusing and counterproductive.

As beneficial as such relationships can be for all parties, they are time-consuming and can become overwhelming. If such a surrogate is unaware or unprepared, he or she may find it necessary to discourage the relationship and to create distance between her or himself and you, the survivor. This person who has become a surrogate may still find you an attractive and appealing person, but she or he may not have the time or energy—for reasons that have nothing to do with you—to maintain the level of energy and commitment demanded of such a relationship. Even though the person may employ the most cautious and tactful efforts to discourage the excessive attachment that has developed and create a more balanced and healthy relationship, you may experience these efforts as another form of disapproval and rejection. Once again you believe you are being told you are not worthy of acceptance and affection. You are being told something is wrong with you. This is not in any way your friend's feeling or intention, but it is what you feel.

As painful as the process of redefining and clarifying the proper nature of a relationship may be, it is critical that you as a survivor learn to develop appropriate and healthy relationships. You must acknowledge and continually remind yourself of the source of the strong need you have for acceptance and approval. You must remind yourself that there are many ways to gain acceptance and many people from whom to receive it. This person is not the only one from whom it is possible to receive love. As difficult as you may sometimes find it to believe, there are, in fact, many people who find you attractive, appealing, and worthwhile. You must remind yourself that because someone is not always as responsive as you might like or need, this lack of response does not constitute a rejection of you as a person. The lack of responsiveness may be the result of the person's own lack of ability or because of other demands on his or her time. It is not—and I cannot emphasize this enough—because you are worthless.

Truth Shall Be Found in Testing

The second kind of reaction that your poor self-esteem may create to the acceptance and approval you receive from other people is disbelief and distrust. You may feel attracted to any person or group that says you are worthwhile and lovable, but you feel suspicious and skeptical. For you such approval is gratifying but disconcerting. You are constantly wondering, "Is it real? Will it last?" You are sure that there must be some mistake. You cannot be comfortable with what is happening or relax and bask in the glow of being loved. You live with the abiding fear that the approval will soon stop.

You may also experience receiving approval as what some survivors describe as having the first shoe drop. The second shoe falls when that approval is withdrawn and you again are told you are worthless and useless. The one constant in your family was that approval was never constant. It was always subject to being revoked, always open to being rescinded. When the anxiety of waiting for the second shoe became too much, you sometimes may have felt compelled to make it fall. You began to bait and test those who were giving you approval. Even today your expectation of rejection prompts you to examine every statement of approval for a sign of insincerity or inconsistency. You question and challenge any sign of approval. You test and probe and scrutinize.

For a person who is your friend such constant testing can become aggravating. The other person begins to feel that he is always being examined. No statement is ever taken at face value. Every question is asked in three different ways to see if the same answer is forthcoming. Questions that your friend thought had been put to rest long ago are resurrected to see if the answer has been revised. You are certain that any approval you have received is open to being rescinded, and you feel compelled to check constantly to determine the status of your acceptance. In our support groups this meant that old issues frequently were brought up in new guises to see if the leaders' responses were the same. It also meant that any time members shared new information about themselves the leaders were always asked, "Do you still like me?"

One of my coleaders has kept in touch with a former group member for several years. She is still asked regularly, "Do you still like me?" If the slightest hint of annoyance creeps into the coleader's response, the former group member hears it as a sign of rejection. Such constant testing can put a strain on a relationship and test the patience of a saint.

Not all your friends may be saints. You must work to accept their acceptance. As difficult as it may be, you must swallow your questions and believe you are loved. As strange as it may seem, this is not easy. You learned to distrust those closest to you through many years of brutally ingrained training. To learn a different lesson will also take time and practice. Be gentle and patient with yourself!

Manipulation as Survival

Such constant questioning and testing is a form of manipulation. It is your way as a survivor of controlling the relationship between yourself and the giver of approval. You are trying to determine what response or ways of acting will get people to accept you. Such manipulation is annoying and revolting to someone accustomed to dealing honestly and directly with people. Most people get angry when they feel they are being manipulated. They feel someone is trying to put something over on them or trying to get them to do something they do not really want to do. Manipulation may also mean someone is trying to get something fraudulently. In most cases people are manipulative when they are trying to get something they do not deserve or get out of something they do deserve. The common response is to try to thwart such behavior.

Such a response to manipulation is understandable and is an appropriate way to act except when one is dealing with survivors. As a survivor you were not accustomed to dealing with people directly. Your family situation was so chaotic and the forms of communication so convoluted that you were always required to assess and question the motives and intentions of your family members. Roles were not clearly defined. Expectations were never voiced. Requests were not made directly. Your parents seldom responded directly to the needs you expressed as a child. Therefore, if you wanted anything you had to find indirect, manipulative ways to attain them. You were forced to manipulate your parents in order to get approval and to have your basic need for affection met. This was often true even of your most basic human needs.

For you as a survivor, manipulation was the only way you had
to get what you needed and deserved and to avoid being beaten
and ridiculed. You had to cover up mother's drinking so that your
father would not beat her or you. You had to learn to say only
what your father wanted to hear so you would be allowed to have
dinner. You had to respond to your uncle's sexual requests so he
would not fulfill his threats to harm you or your brothers and
sisters. You learned at a young age to know what people around
you wanted and to respond quickly in order to avoid trouble and
to receive any modicum of approval. This was manipulation; it
was game playing, but it was necessary for survival.

Such manipulative responses are automatic and unconscious
for you as a survivor. You are not even aware that your actions are
manipulative. You are not being malicious. As you become aware
of what you are doing, you must avoid moral judgments of
yourself.

Yet even as moral judgments are avoided, corrective action
must be taken. While acknowledging that your abusive background may have taught you to deal with your parents in this
way, you must constantly remind yourself that you are not
dealing with your family. You are, in most cases, working with
people who are forthright in their relationships and will attempt
to respond to your needs in whatever ways are possible for them.
You must seek to foster new experiences with other people so you
can apply your learnings about others to different situations. In
this way you can learn that manipulation is no longer necessary
for survival.

Safety in Sensitivity

In order to manipulate people you must be able to read their every
move, to recognize their every desire, and to anticipate their every
need before it is stated. These are skills that you as a survivor
learned early.

On one occasion, my coleader confessed to me after a meeting
that she had had a particularly bad day and was in a bad mood.
She hoped it had not shown in the meeting. I assured her that I
had not really noticed. Therefore, I was sure that the group
members had not noticed. At the beginning of the next meeting,
I discovered how wrong I had been. All of the members of the

group had noticed and had compared notes between meetings. They wanted to know what had been wrong because they needed to make sure it was not something they had done.

This incident was exceptional only because of the way the group handled it. They actually confronted my coleader and tried to deal with the issues involved. More typically, they would have identified a problem, assumed it was their fault, and then would have tried to avoid it. In this instance, some of the members met by chance during the week and compared their impressions. They realized they shared a common perception and this gave them the courage to bring up the issue. Such a process is the exception rather than the rule.

Usually, instead of using their highly developed sensitivity to the moods and feelings of others as means to establish stronger more intimate relationships, survivors use these skills as tools to avoid conflicts and potentially emotional situations. They recognize potential conflicts early, then work frantically to avoid rather than confront and resolve them.

This is a natural reaction since the context and the manner in which you as a survivor developed your skills were in situations that frequently resulted in violence. You learned to recognize the moods and feelings of your parents or abusive spouses in order to protect yourself. It was essential that you quickly determine whether your father was in a good or bad mood the moment he walked in the room so that you would know whether to run to greet him or run to hide, whether you could talk about what happened at school or whether you should quietly bury yourself in the corner with a book, whether you could talk and joke with your husband or quickly and quietly put dinner on the table. Thus, you learned quickly and well the telltale signs that indicate a person's mood—whether the shoulders were hunched or straight, the face relaxed or tense, the hands open or clenched. You learned to read all of these signs instantly and instinctively. You learned to do it without thinking and without realizing you were doing it. This skill is as important and natural a part of your life as eating and drinking—and just as important for your survival.

Thus, you developed a finely tuned interpersonal skill, the ability to be sensitive to others. There is a problem, however. This skill was learned as a defense mechanism, as a way to protect yourself. It was not learned as a means of interpersonal intimacy or as a way to get to know people better. You mastered it as a way to recognize the danger signals and to know when to protect yourself, to escape, to change the subject, or to do whatever was expected of you. Therefore, this skill, which counselors and psychologists spend long hours and lots of money learning, became your instinctive response to all people in all situations. It became an unconscious part of the way you relate to others. Your first reaction to people is to determine what their mood is and what they might want. Thus, your instinctive response is to determine how to meet the needs of other people or to escape from situations so that you will not be attacked. By these methods you learned to keep yourself safe.

Despite the finely tuned nature of this interpersonal skill, you did not learn to form true interpersonal relationships. Instead of developing reciprocal relationships, you focused on the needs of others to the exclusion of your own. The primary purpose for such a focus was to protect yourself from someone who might not be in a good mood, not to understand and help that person.

Since every person has an occasional bad day, this ability to be sensitive to the moods of others and the defensive nature of its application means that as a survivor you often do not form close friendships. Sometimes you may be attracted to someone, but when you detect that the person is having a bad day you begin to avoid him, because you believe it must be the result of something you did and because you fear the bad mood will mean that the person will become violent towards you. You fear that your friend will turn on you and will treat you like your parents did when they had had a bad day.

This creates a change in the relationship. The potential friend becomes confused and disenchanted. She does not understand why you are suddenly avoiding her or are so distant when you are together. Your friend understandably becomes impatient with the erratic nature of the relationship and may decide to quit trying to make it work. You have inadvertently destroyed a relationship because of your misapplication of a skill that should have made the relationship more intimate. Because of your deeply ingrained fears, your ability to be sensitive to the moods and needs of a friend have proven to be a liability rather than an asset.

If your friends are aware that you are an abuse survivor, they can be aware of your defensive tendency to be sensitive to the moods of other people. They can be very explicit about their moods when dealing with you and be careful to explain why they are having a bad day—and that it has nothing to do with you. They can also be aware when you are misapplying your sensitivity to them. In such instances, understanding friends can intervene by helping you understand what is really happening. Such interventions require a great deal of sensitivity and patience on the part of a friend. It also demands that you as the survivor be clear with your friends about your abuse and how it is affecting you. This takes a great deal of self-understanding and courage, but it can be a great help to you as you strive to develop supportive relationships with your friends. Both you and your friends can grow from such a process.

On the other hand, you need to recognize the inappropriateness of your behavior and seek to change it. You must work to adjust your constantly defensive posture. You should not seek to blunt your sensitivity—that is not desirable because not everybody out there is concerned about your welfare. However, you must acknowledge that you are highly sensitive and that you apply the information such sensitivity provides in an overly defensive manner. You must constantly remind yourself that not everyone is out to hurt you. You do not need to react with fear to everyone's thoughtless and distressful mood. You may need to confront your fear and take a risk when approaching a disgruntled friend to ask what is wrong. In most cases you will find that talking with a friend who is in such a mood can open up new aspects of your relationship.

Excessive Control

This extreme sensitivity to the needs of others is one way by which you as a survivor strive to control your environment. As we discussed earlier, as an abuse victim you learned early that you had little control over your life. Your parents were inconsistent in their reactions to you, and you did not learn what actions to perform to achieve desired outcomes. You were also given few opportunities to make decisions about your life. You were told what to do and severely punished when you did anything other than what your parents wanted of you. Therefore, you seek every possible way to limit the negative influences in your life since every person or incident is seen as potentially harmful. You seek to limit any form of contact that can be harmful, keeping relationships to a minimum. You avoid outside contacts as much as possible and limit the possibilities of what might happen in relationships with others. In short, you strive to have as much control as possible.

This can be frustrating to people with whom you may be dealing. Friends want to have more frequent contacts, to engage in new kinds of activities. You, on the other hand, want to keep such things at a minimum so the possibilities for negative experiences can also be held to a minimum. New experiences are a threat to you. They constitute an encounter with something with which you have little or no familiarity. Since your assumption is that new experiences are going to be negative, it is safer to avoid them than to try anything new. Every new experience is perceived as an opportunity for disaster. It is better to make sure nothing new happens than to have something happen that could turn out to be unsafe. It is better to have a severely limited—but at least safe—environment than one with opportunities that will certainly be filled with harm and disaster as well. Such limiting of experiences deters the freedom and spontaneity necessary for you to develop satisfying relationships with others.

This lack of spontaneity and controlling approach to life is not just related to your external activities. It can also be the pattern for your approach to your emotions. You may control your emotional expressions so completely that they are practically nonexistent. Your willingness and ability to share your feelings is severely limited. Once again this is something you learned early in life. You learned it was not safe to express your emotions because they were met with abuse. This lack of emotional response is so common among very young abused children that social workers have given it a name—"frozen watchfulness." Social workers observed that many abused children were extremely restrained in their response to normally emotional situations. Such children would sit quietly for long periods without any visible response. However, the social workers observed that they were fully aware of what was happening around them and prepared to respond instantly in defense.

Such excessive control of emotions can also be very frustrating for persons who may be trying to relate to you. Your discomfort with emotions and your inability to share feelings makes it difficult for a prospective friend to get to know you and your needs and preferences. Friends are unable to determine what pleases you, excites you, encourages you, or distresses you. Thus, your friends must guess what you want to do for an evening or what completely turns you off. You learned long ago that your desires were not important and that your needs would not be met or, in fact, would often be directly contradicted. Therefore, it was safer not to express needs, not to acknowledge preferences, and not to ask for anything. After years of active denial you have ceased to be conscious of even having needs and desires. When asked what you would like to do, how you feel about something or what someone can do to help you, your "I don't know" is an accurate description of your level of personal awareness. It does express what you know about your personal desires.

As accurate as such a statement may be, it is still frustrating for a person attempting to get to know you. It is still trying to the patience of a friend. Your excessive control stifles your own creativity and joy and blocks your ability to be yourself at the same time that it contravenes your friend's desires and efforts to establish meaningful communication and sharing. It frustrates friendship.

Comfort with Chaos

Even though you may strive valiantly to control your emotions and achieve control over the circumstances of your life, you may nevertheless exhibit a great affinity for chaos. One of the few predictable factors in an abusive family is its inconsistency and chaos. Little structure or order exists, family roles are frequently shifted, and personal expectations and demands constantly change. Such confusion, as disruptive and destructive as it may be, was the experience most familiar to you as a survivor. It was the mode of operation with which you were familiar. It is also the manner of relating to people you know best and it is the one with which you are most comfortable.

Therefore, you may lack the ability to concentrate for long on a single task or to complete an assignment. You may not understand the importance of bringing topics of conversation to satisfactory conclusions, and you may have no sense of how to plan the details of events and actions. You may lack any notion of what it means to establish priorities and to act according to them. Such processes are foreign to your experience. You do not understand how to focus your attention and plan for contingencies, and you do not even know why it is important to do so. You do not know what all the fuss is about. Isn't it better to just hang loose; everything will work out—as well as anything ever does. Such an approach will drive well-organized people absolutely bananas, but as a survivor you cannot understand why there is a problem.

Another dimension to this problem is that for many survivors experiencing a structured environment is not only difficult, it is frightening. For many of you, the only time attention in your families was focused was when violence was being directed at someone. The only time you knew someone was paying attention to you was when you were being yelled at or abused. The only time there was any evidence that people cared about you was when they got angry. In such circumstances, the experience of having someone's undivided attention was a threatening and painful experience, and it meant you were going to be hit or ridiculed.

Thus, a chaotic, nonfocused environment is safer because it means that no one—especially you—is being abused. You are actually more comfortable with chaos because you feel the likelihood of violence is lessened when many things are happening at the same time. If there is little plan or forethought to events, if there is no schedule that anyone is expected to follow, then there is less possibility that anyone will become upset. But even if someone is upset, you cannot be blamed that "things didn't turn out."

This may have been an effective way to avoid violence in your family, but it drives anyone crazy who is not operating from such a background or from such premises. Other people cannot understand why you do not plan for events, get nervous when someone suggests that you plan, do not follow plans that are made, and seem to undermine all efforts at planning and rationality.

One way to change this disruptive behavior is to become active in structured groups where the agenda is firmly controlled. You may feel some resistance and discomfort with this experience, but if you are able to control your propensity for chaos, you will appreciate and learn from the experience. In such a setting you can become more conscious about trying to change your behavior and can learn that such avoidance behavior is not necessary in nonabusive environments.

Lying in Order to Survive

Much of what we have just discussed may seem to say that what you as a survivor do verges on the immoral—you manipulate and maneuver people; you may not be fully honest. The fact of the matter is, you were brought up with a set of expectations and in an environment that required you to protect yourself by methods that may not necessarily be considered moral.

As important as virtues are, their formation presupposes reciprocity and happens best in a supportive environment. In your violent family you did not experience such reinforcement. You did not experience loving parents or supportive families. Your experience did not encourage honesty or reward loyalty. For you certain virtues were not the "norm" for your life. In order to survive you learned habits that are contrary to basic moral principles.

One of the moral codes commonly violated in an abusive family is that of honesty. A culture of deception surrounds family violence in our society, a culture developed within the family but encouraged and enhanced by society as a whole. Deception and deceit were taught in your family when your parents told you not to talk about the abuse that was happening. Even if you were not told to keep quiet, you were terrified of what might happen if you did tell. Deceit became the basis for survival when you knew that if you told what was happening, you or other members of your family would be punished. Deception became a way of life when your abusive husband told you not to report him, "If you know what's good for you," or when you heard your mother tell friends there was nothing wrong and that her bruises were the result of an accident. You learned that lying is a way of life—you were trained to lie.

The range of the deceptive culture expanded when violence was condemned in society, but people looked the other way and ignored abuse when they saw it happening around them. They preferred not to get involved. The deception became ingrained when accusations about abuse were rejected without proper investigation and when victims paid higher personal prices than the perpetrators themselves; for example, as a child you were removed from your home—"for your own good"—while your abusive parent remained.

You learned a distorted sense of truth when your father told you that nothing was wrong even though mother drinks a lot, burns food, and falls down. Confusion abounded when Uncle Harry was greeted as a favorite relative even though he did things that were supposed to be "not nice." The distortion became overwhelming when your mother left you alone for long periods of time with your sexually abusive father and then snickered and made snide comments about "Daddy's favorite little girl."

You learned that lying was a preferred way of life when your parents' demands were so unrealistic and inflexible that the only way you could live up to them was by covering up failures. You wisely chose to lie when your parents' responses to mistakes were so violent that the only way to avoid beatings was to lie when mistakes were made. Lying was preferred to truth when truth about your family could result in investigations that might break up the family and put you in juvenile hall or a foster home.

You learned to question your perception of reality, your ability to distinguish truth from falsehood, when your experience of violence in your home was contrary to the public reputation of the family. You questioned your own sanity when your attempts to solicit help resulted in disbelief, accusations of troublemaking, or referral for psychiatric treatment. Under such circumstances, you learned that the deception required to preserve an appearance of family stability and family cohesion was preferred to truth. In such situations you learned to adjust your concept of your family in order to maintain a sense of rationality and sanity.

Sometimes your perception of reality about your family became so distorted and your experience of family life so far out of sync with the images communicated within society that you were not able to reconcile your images and your experience with any sense of integrity. You lived with constant confusion about what constituted truth and reality in your life.

Even if you were able to understand the truth about the violent realities of your family life, you soon discovered that the effort required to express that truth carried a great price. The price of truthfulness was more than you could bear. The cost involved personal pain, parental rejection, and family dissolution—and as chaotic, disruptive, and distorted as your family may have been, it was the only family you had. You did not know what you would do if you lost it.

Such training in deception easily extended to other areas of life and to other relationships. Having learned such distortions in your family you may have similarly confused perceptions of what is good or bad and true or false in the broader world. If you could not figure out what was real in your family, how can you trust your perceptions about other persons, situations, or groups? If deception was a recommended course of action in your family, why should it not be used in other relationships? If certain things were to be concealed in your family life, are there not similar things to be concealed in the rest of the world? If some topics were forbidden or not safe in one circumstance, what makes them okay in another? This thinking is the natural result of the family training you received, training that has created immense confusion about reality and truth. You have lived with distortion so long you can no longer distinguish truth from falsehood.

When you now try to tell the truth, you may experience confusion about what really is true. You may experience anxiety and even guilt because you fear you are telling something that you are not supposed to, that you are going to get yourself or someone else in trouble. Thus for you, honesty is not the best policy; it has too many negative ramifications.

I am not condoning lying or suggesting that you continue to succumb to the culture of deception in which you were raised. However, I am acknowledging that to expect you to respond instantly to moral exhortations for truthfulness is unrealistic. Any exhortation in favor of honesty must be accompanied by acknowledgement of the confusion that you may be experiencing and a recognition of the anxiety that may be attached to such an act. You also need assistance in understanding that the responses you will receive from authority figures at this time will be different from the responses you got from your parents. You need assistance in learning to sort out truth from falsehood and in convincing yourself that the truth is not going to result in tremendous personal cost. You need to be convinced that honesty is not going to result in ridicule and beatings and that sharing problems is not going to bring rejection. You need to *experience* that honesty is the best policy.

You must also remind yourself that your propensity for dishonesty is not malicious; it is an act you think necessary for survival. However, it is not an act that continues to be necessary indefinitely. You are no longer living in dangerous circumstances or operating in a volatile environment where a misstatement or an unacceptable response will result in violence.

When attempting to convince yourself that you no longer need to lie for protection, you are proposing to give up one of your best instruments of self-preservation. You are not trying to overcome a weakness but to throw out one of your strongest skills. Such time-tested tools are not going to be relinquished without a struggle. You must convince yourself that the tool is no longer necessary or that it will not work in normal, nonabusive situations.

You learned that lying was a very effective tool for survival. It was the best way to protect yourself and to win the game of life. Good intentions alone are not going to convince you to give up your winning advantage. You must also come to realize that it is no longer necessary, and that it is not an effective way to win at life. It antagonizes other people and undermines their trust in you. It destroys relationships that are based on honesty and trust.

You need to develop a new repertoire of ways to relate to other people in order to function at a new level of human proficiency. You must learn new strategies for dealing with others. You need to choose to stop lying, to risk honest relationships, and to practice such behavior repeatedly. You will find that the relationships based on deception will change or be lost, but your life and relationships will be much easier and more fulfilling. Then the culture of deception, which has ruled your life, will be broken and you will learn to function in a culture of honesty. The task may be difficult but it is possible and the choice is yours.

Inappropriate Reactions

The kinds of behaviors we have been discussing are clearly inappropriate to those who grew up in well-functioning families. Such reactions are dysfunctional, counterproductive, and disruptive. The following examples of dysfunction, drawn from accounts provided by members of Grown-Up Abused Children groups, exhibit the range of dysfunction that can be generated by abuse and suggest things you may need to watch for or which can help you understand and revise some of your own inappropriate reactions.

You who in the past or even now experience violence in your families may have many different situations to which you have negative or even frightening reactions. These situations may trigger anxiety toward something that would not normally be considered threatening. They may trigger hostile responses to situations or to the comments of others that would normally be considered innocuous, inoffensive, or even encouraging.

Some of the examples given earlier have referred to the kinds of reactions survivors have had to situations that consciously or subconsciously reminded them of circumstances from their past. We have discussed the problems you as a survivor may have with touching or being touched. Whether it is a gentle pat on the back or a friendly hug, such physical contact can strike terror in your heart and cause you to react with startled withdrawal or freeze with fear. You may also experience nausea. Such responses confuse those who observe you and may lead others to brand you as "strange." These behaviors may also convince a prospective friend that you do not want to have a relationship with him or her. Of course, such is not the case, but your reaction has communicated that message.

Another example of an inappropriate reaction happened in a Grown-up Abused Children group. A male member was particularly soft-spoken. Frequently, group members would ask him to speak louder. Invariably he would become angry after such encouragement and refuse to talk at all. This happened several times before we were able to get him to explain the reasons for his anger. At one meeting, after much pressure, he finally blurted it out: "You people are just like my father. You are always making fun of the way I talk."

The explanation for his outburst was that he had not learned to talk until he was almost four years old. His family members, especially his father, ridiculed him for this and his speech became a continuing subject of family derision. As a result, he became very sensitive to any comments about his speech. Therefore, even comments intended to encourage him to express his ideas were interpreted as negative and demeaning. Only after extensive discussion in the group was he able to understand the difference between encouraging comments about his speech and those intended to ridicule.

Another example is a woman who reported feeling extremely anxious whenever she saw an aquarium. While visiting a pet shop one day with a friend who was purchasing tropical fish for her son, her anxiety became overwhelming. She got so nervous she almost fainted. Fortunately, her friend recognized that something was wrong, got her out of the pet store, and found a place where they could talk. As they discussed her anxiety, she became aware of her first recollection of aquariums. Her father had several in his den. Then she recalled that her father had sexually abused her as a small child and that his aquariums had been the only thing she had to look at while he was attacking her.

She had completely blocked the sexual abuse and had transferred her anxiety to the aquariums. Once she made the connections, she not only began to enjoy tropical fish, but more importantly, she was able to deal constructively with the effects of the sexual abuse as they were manifested in her relationships with others, especially men.

As these few examples indicate, the situations to which you as a survivor may have inappropriate reactions are extremely diverse and difficult to predict. Adverse reactions can arise in the most innocuous situations. Very ordinary situations or objects create startling and disturbing reactions. It is difficult for most nonsurvivors to understand these connections between past circumstances and present events. The experiences you may have had as a survivor were often so bizarre and different from the experiences of others that friends find them difficult to comprehend, despite your best explanations and their best intentions.

The important thing to remember is that if you discover yourself having unusual reactions to commonplace events and situations, you should consider these matters worth investigating. They may contain clues to aspects of your abuse that can help you in your healing and growing. All people have experiences from their past that color and affect the way they perceive the present. Fortunately, most of those are positive. They provide insights and skills that help people understand, analyze, and creatively respond to present events.

As a survivor you had experiences that gave you false information and maladaptive skills. You had negative experiences with situations that are normally positive. Your experiences may have been so brutal that you blocked the details of the event from your memory; all you have in your consciousness is your reaction to specific stimuli. These stimuli (for example, aquariums) re-create the anxiety, the pain, and the defense reactions associated with the original event—but without recollections of the event itself.

You may have large periods of your life for which you have no memories and images of violence and pain for which you have no explanation. Such experiences coupled with bizarre reactions to commonplace objects and events are the result of your severe trauma. They are symptoms of a diagnosis known as Post-Traumatic Stress Disorder (PTSD), a problem that has received a lot of publicity because of its prevalence among Vietnam veterans. We will discuss this at greater length in the next chapter. Persons experiencing extreme stress block many of their physical reactions and emotional feelings in order to survive either physically or emotionally. Having blocked these events from their conscious memory, some parts of the experience may reappear at seemingly unconnected and irrational moments. Just as the blocking was part of the defense process, the recollections and images are part of the healing process. They are part of the psyche's effort to reintegrate the traumatic event in one's life.

When such processes occur, you should not dismiss the seemingly irrational and inappropriate reactions you may have or your experiences of unexplainable images and visions of violence as the product of the craziness your parents always ascribed to you. Such occurrences may be the work of your strong personality, which has survived extreme trauma and is now striving to regain its full health. Taking these accounts seriously and seeking help from counselors who understand abuse and PTSD can help you understand this admittedly bizarre behavior and can reassure you that you are not "losing your mind" or hallucinating, and can help you regain your memories and reintegrate the parts of your life that you have lost.

It has always amazed me to observe how clarifications about single, small events in a survivor's life can result in significant changes in the way she or he responds to situations and relates to

people. Such insights can improve a person's effectiveness, pro-
ductivity, and happiness. It can happen for you.

It is impossible to identify all the circumstances to which you
may have irrational reactions or exhibit inappropriate behaviors.
Your life—as well as everyone else's—is so diverse and complex
that the possibilities are infinite. The variations possible within
the forms of abuse we have discussed, the variations possible
because of the different ages at which abuse may have begun and
ended, and the kinds of supports that may or may not have been
available make the forms and intensity of your betraying behaviors impossible to predict.

The examples and the explanations in this chapter are provided
to give you some hints about what to look for so you can be more
understanding and sensitive to your own needs as a survivor. This
knowledge can help you recognize the reasons for these betraying
behaviors, support you in your struggle, and give you the skills you
need to develop new, healthier responses to the world around
you. These insights can also help friends and family members
acquire that extra bit of patience needed to look beyond the
bizarre, confusing, and even infuriating behaviors of their survivor friends. Then they will be able to support and guide you as you
grow beyond the distortions created by your violent past. Then
you can experience the joy of a God who is "a God not of disorder
but of peace" (1 Cor. 14:33).

5 | Dreaming Dreams to See Visions

For many the God of peace is a long way off. The peace of mind so often promised and exalted by preachers may be absent from your life. Instead, the confusion of disturbing and disruptive memories plagues your mind. Fleeting images during the day, as well as dreams at night, are a continuing source of distress. Images from your past become confused with experiences in the present. Your life feels like a cauldron of confusion and hopelessness.

Anger is also boiling within you, robbing you of any peace. You are angry about what was done to you, angry at the people who hurt you, and angry about the physical pain you suffered and the emotional pain you continue to experience. You may even be angry at the God who allowed you to be abused and at the people—some of them religious leaders—who allowed it to go on and even suggested that it was your fault or that you shouldn't be angry and that you should "forgive and forget," "Honor your father and your mother," or "Be subject to your husband."

Such emotions and confusion make virtues seem remote, prayer painful, and reconciliation repulsive. You want to forget your past, but you cannot. You are too hurt and angry to even think about forgiving. Anxiety and fear are the ruling factors in your life, not confidence and peace.

Given the pain of your abuse and the continuing problems it can cause, it is not uncommon for you to repress and deny many of your experiences. They were too painful; they were too disorienting to be allowed fully into consciousness. If you had allowed yourself to feel fully the pain and anguish, you would have been totally overwhelmed. Therefore, you continually tried to push them from your memory.

William Sloane Coffin once graphically pointed out that the digestive system of the human psyche does not have an elimination canal: "What goes down must come up" (1981). As much as you may want to forget and as effectively as you may have blocked your experiences in order to survive, the memory of these experiences all too frequently pop back up at unusual, unexpected, and embarrassing times. Often such recollections come unannounced and without warning. Frequently they seem to lack any association with reality. The memories that suddenly appear are not about anything of which you have any previous recollection. You have images of being physically beaten or sexually abused— incidents of which you have no conscious memory.

You may have physical sensations of discomfort and even nausea at various times and in certain situations, but you may not remember anything. Your body seems to be telling you something, but you do not remember abuse, neither do you remember pleasant times. As has been said, for many survivors large blocks of their lives are lost; they have no recollections. If you are in this category remembering is an even more difficult process. Your only key is your subconscious.

The beginning of your recollection process can be found in your dreams or in flashbacks and fleeting images you experience while awake. These dreams or flashbacks may contain sexually or physically violent images or explicit incidents that you do not consciously recollect. Frequently, you may discount these experiences as hallucinations. Often therapists also discount such images as hallucinations or Freudian fantasies.

However, such unexpected memories and fleeting images often offer clues to specific forms of abuse or particularly violent episodes of abuse for persons who are already aware that they were abused. Many members of Grown-Up Abused Children groups initially remember experiences of physical abuse but have no recollection of sexual abuse. After time in a group, some persons begin to recall and reexperience the incidents of sexual abuse. The strength and insight they gain about their physical abuse enables them to deal with the realities of their sexual abuse.

Someone has said, "Our memories are gentle." They allow us to remember only what we have the ability to handle.

Such memories and flashbacks can also be the key to understanding early forms of abuse that happened almost before you could cognitively define them. Such sensory images are reports about what "the bones remember." As painful as these recollections are, they are signs of health. As a survivor you begin to have such memories when you are strong enough to know how to deal with these realities out of your past. Your psyche can finally allow you to remember. You can remember without being totally overwhelmed—as overwhelming as such experiences may seem at first. You may need help to integrate this new information into your adult life, but you are taking an important step toward putting your life back together.

As such memories flood and sometimes seem to overwhelm your consciousness, it is important to remind yourself that these are not new experiences for you. They are memories; they are recollections of past events that you have already survived. As painful and frightening as the images may be, they are not real and they are about events that you already successfully endured at a time when you had fewer resources with which to manage the painful realities. As difficult as managing these memories may be, the fact that you survived the previous violence means you can persist through the reliving of the past images.

Another way that past abusive experiences are regurgitated from the psychological digestive system is through strange and unexplained phobias. One woman returned to the group after the holidays. She had spent Christmas Day with friends. As they were seated around the dinner table, she became so anxious that she had to leave the table. She said, "I don't know what caused this, but I am sure it has some relationship to my abuse." As we discussed the incident, we also began to discuss the dining patterns of her family. She soon realized that she always sat to the left of her father at dinner and he frequently hit her viciously, knocking her out of her chair. At the Christmas dinner she had been seated to the left of a male guest. The similarity to her family situation was subconsciously so threatening she had to leave. She ended the discussion by saying, "Now that I know why I felt so anxious I think I can control it in the future. Before I didn't know what was going on with me so I couldn't make myself distinguish the present from the past."

It is important for you as a survivor to pay close attention to these phobias and flashbacks. As much as you may prefer to do so, you must not write them off as hallucinations or as another example of the craziness so often attributed to you by your parents. You must examine these images for important sources of information about your past and ways in which they influence your present.

These images are the first signs of a past seeking to be recalled, forgotten experiences striving to be remembered, and traumatic incidents begging to be recognized. These images are part of what psychological researchers call "intrusive recollections" of a traumatic event (Diagnostic and Statistical Manual [DSM] III 1980, 236)—one of the characteristic symptoms of PTSD.

PTSD is a clinical diagnostic category that recognizes that a survivor of trauma may reexperience "elements of the trauma in dreams, uncontrollable and emotionally distressing intrusive images and dissociative mental states." A survivor also experiences "a loss of normal affect and emotional responsiveness, and exhibits less interest and involvement in work and interpersonal relationships" (Green 1981, 3). These two characteristics may coexist or occur in cycles.

These reactions are common in persons who have experienced a "recognizable stressor that would evoke significant symptoms of distress in almost everyone" (DSM III 1980, 238). Such "stressors" can range from natural disasters (tornadoes and floods) to accidental human-made disasters (car accidents, fires) and deliberate human-made disasters (bombings, torture, military combat, and child abuse), which produce trauma outside normal experience.

Several factors affect the severity of a person's reaction: "The disorder is apparently more severe and longer lasting when the stressor is of human design" (DSM III 1980, 236). The severity of the response is also "dependent in large part on the nature and intensity of the individual's personal experience of a traumatic event" (Green 1981, 10). "The specific meaning of the event to an individual . . . [is also] a factor in the working through process" (Green 1981, 12).

Certainly family violence ranks high as a "recognizable stressor outside of normal experience." It also contains factors that intensify the disorder. It is of human design, it is intensely personal, and most batterers attach specific messages about their victim's personal meaning and value to the blows they inflict.

As a victim of family violence you also lacked a key ingredient that could have helped you adapt to the effects of the stress and integrate the experience into a healthy perception of reality—a supportive environment. What should have been your principal source of support—your family—was instead the source of your trauma. Often when your abuse was revealed, even the parts of your family that provided some small source of stability disintegrated. If you sought aid and were rejected, the disorders caused by the severe stress were compounded.

You may have experienced a number of stress reactions immediately after you were abused, such as anxiety, inability to sleep, and nightmares. On the other hand, you may have experienced no unusual reactions or may have no recollection of the event. Weeks, months, or even years later you may begin to reexperience the trauma. This may manifest itself as follows:

(1) Recurrent and intrusive recollections of the event
(2) Recurrent dreams of the event
(3) Sudden acting or feeling as if the traumatic event were recurring, because of an association with an environmental or ideational stimulus.

You also may recognize new psychological symptoms:

(1) Hyperalertness or exaggerated startle response
(2) Sleep disturbance
(3) Guilt about surviving when others have not, or about behavior required for survival
(4) Memory impairment or trouble concentrating
(5) Avoidance of activities that arouse recollection of the traumatic event
(6) Intensification of symptoms by exposure to events that symbolize or resemble the traumatic event (DSM III 1980, 238).

These are the signs that your traumatic event is striving to reassert itself. The denial, which may have been necessary for you to survive and manage the psychic overload from your intense or outrageous experience, is beginning to break down. As critical as those defenses were when you developed them, you are now in a place where you no longer need them. As implausible as it may seem because of the discomfort you are experiencing, this break-down constitutes a sign of health. Your psyche is recognizing that you have developed new strengths, which enable you to face your trauma and work it through to an integrated view of the world and of yourself. Now new information can become an integral part of your personality.

In this phase of achieving solidarity with your pain you not only begin to acknowledge the traumatic past but also to confront the maladaptive behaviors that have been a part of your defense system. You may now recognize that your use of chemicals, your fantasy about and attempts at suicide, or your phobic avoidance of situations that remind you of the trauma are no longer needed. You may also experience relief from the depression and "psychic numbing" that have ruled your life. You can relax your compulsive efforts to manipulate and control those around you as you learn to trust other people and allow them to show their caring in their own unique way.

Since the key to healing for sufferers from PTSD (in this instance, survivors of family violence) is movement from denial to recognition and integration, the experience of intrusive images in the form of unexplainable dreams and flashbacks is a positive part of the process. Such experiences are a natural and important part of your healing process. You must foster rather than resist these images and follow them to their natural conclusions.

The process of working with these intrusive images is the same as that for dealing with the vague and incoherent recollections we discussed above. The images need to be examined in detail. With the help of a counselor you must focus on the pieces of information that are available and strive to reconstruct the details of the original experience.

An important caution should be noted here. Your efforts to reconstruct the details should not be done alone. You should restrict efforts to reconstruct the traumatic experience to times when a trusted friend or counselor is available. You may need support, reassurance, and even control when going through such an experience. Part of the nature of PTSD is that reliving the trauma can be a total sensory experience. All the past sights, smells, and feelings can recur. This can be frightening, painful, and disorienting. You may forget where you are and act in a bizarre fashion. In addition to the problems associated with reliving the event, you may become emotionally disoriented. Recalling the experience may add a whole new dimension to your life that may require a redefinition of yourself and the reality of your family and world. A supportive and understanding counselor will be essential in such circumstances.

This process is not easy. It can be so painful and disconcerting that it would seem better to avoid the whole thing. Such difficulties provide a good rationale for blocking the process and for continuing to avoid your pain.

In reality such blocking cannot be done. The flashbacks and intrusive images will keep coming until they are dealt with and resolved. On the other hand, "successful" denial leads to unsuccessful conduct. Common maladaptive behaviors that may help you hide the reality of your trauma include depression, drug abuse, suicide, and behavior destructive to personal relationships—the many behaviors we have discussed. Such behavior disrupts your personal peace and detracts from the wholeness of your life.

You have a vision of what you want your life to be and what it means to be whole, to experience caring family relationships, and to live at peace. As contradictory as it may seem, your disturbing dreams and unwanted images are important steps toward attaining that vision. By reliving the pain, you can relieve your anxieties, resolve your conflicts, and reform your relationships. You must undertake the unpleasant and slow but rewarding task of seeking solidarity with your pain so you can attain your vision.

Achieving Solidarity with Your Pain

If you lived in a violent family, you did not experience people as trustworthy or life as peaceful. Your life was painful, cruel, and unfair. Therefore, you feel physically, mentally, emotionally, and spiritually stunted, maimed, and deformed. Rather than being hopeful, courageous, and confident, you are frightened, bitter, and frustrated, depressed, angry, and self-deprecating—hardly the basis for a strong, enriching spiritual life.

Achieving solidarity with your pain involves acknowledging the fact that you were abused and neglected by people who should have loved you, in the very place where you should have been safe. It means accepting yourself as a survivor of abuse—with all the hurt and humiliation attached to that. It means stopping all denial about the abuse in your life—whether that is the deep denial involved in blocking all memories or the denial that says, "It wasn't that bad. It didn't/doesn't affect me. It's over, done, and better forgotten." All are ways to avoid accepting the reality of the pain inflicted on you.

However, solidarity with your pain does not mean you blame yourself for your pain or think that what happened to you was in some way your fault. No matter how clumsy a toddler you may have been or how headstrong a teenager, you did not deserve the beatings you received. No matter how cute a preschooler you were or how attractive an adolescent, you were not to blame for your father's sexual behavior.

Certainly your abuser accused you of all manner of infractions, sought to blame you, and looked for excuses for his or her behavior. That was a way of protecting the abuser's own self-image. Maybe you even wanted to believe what happened was in some way your fault. Blaming yourself at least provided some rationality to the chaos of your life. It gave you some sense of power over an uncontrollable situation. If it was your fault, then you have some hope of "fixing" it. Then you had some explanation for your painful and even threatening home life.

Such an explanation is self-destructive and self-defeating. It is an explanation that lays the blame in the wrong place—on you the victim rather than on your parent, spouse, or whoever was the perpetrator. True solidarity with pain enables hope by not accepting repression or condoning the silence and civility that internalize violence and allow perpetrators to go unidentified. Such a conspiracy of silence has allowed family violence to go unchallenged for centuries. Solidarity with pain rejects the inclination to protect the "good names" of community leaders who are also abusers because that impulse robs the victims of self-esteem and hope. It also deprives the abuser of the spiritual opportunity for accountability and change.

Claiming responsibility for your own victimization can also lock you into a never-ending cycle of responsibility. As you tried to make sense out of your abusive home life, you tried everything to "make it better." You were the model, quiet child, you were the perfect student, and you took on major adult responsibilities in your home. You were the constantly responsive, condescending wife. All this was an attempt to "fix your family," to "make things right." When things still became abusive your internal response was, "If only I had/had not. . ." This process of accepting responsibility carries over into adulthood in the form of being the eternal fixer ("If I could just take care of . . . ") or the perfectionist ("If I do this just right, everything will be all right. . ."). Such accepting of responsibility is another form of self-blame that imposes unrealistic expectations, undermines your self-esteem, and continues the abusive pattern in your life.

To be a true person of hope you must recognize the imperfections of your family life and assign responsibility where it belongs—to the persons in power in the relationship. In our society that usually means parents and husbands.

Solidarity with your pain does not mean that you wallow in your pain, that you relish your victim status, or treat yourself as someone to whom that world owes much. Yes, you suffered horribly and unjustly. What was done to you should not have been done to anyone. You deserved better! But the way to achieve better is not to focus on your past suffering but on positive aspects of your present life and on future goals.

Suzanne and Sidney Simon point out in their book, *Forgiveness*, that many people go from "victimization" into "victimhood." They go from acknowledging what happened to them and what was done to them by others to seeing themselves "first and foremost as a victim and living life accordingly." They develop "an attitude, a stance, a way of relating in the world" that is based on "prevailing feelings [they] have about [themselves]" (1990, 125–126). Such people have organized their personalities around being a victim, and it has become a way of life. They spend vast amounts of time feeling sorry for themselves and consoling themselves with food, drugs or shopping sprees (because they deserve it), or taking out their frustrations on those around them. Such behavior is not solidarity with one's pain, it is submerging oneself in one's pain, and it is making oneself a part of the pain. Then you keep "your energy and attention focused on what is missing from your life, [and] life itself passes you by"

(Simon 1990, 138). Such behaviors do not articulate and process the grief that Brueggeman tells us creates hope. They are simply other forms of the repression, civility, and silence that surround the devastating betrayal of family violence.

Yes, you were victimized, but you don't have to live your life as a victim. Yes, things were done to you that you did not deserve, but the important thing now is to live the way you do deserve, in a manner that you desire. As b. f. maiz, a friend, campus ministry colleague, and poet, has written:

> Call grief back,
>   Dear Stranger.
> Paralyze its power to pain,
> Psychoanalyze the clusters
>   of crusted blotches
>   on the winding sheet of the past.
>
> Anesthetize now with normalcy
>   until creativity shocks it down.
> Dear Stranger,
>   mutilate Time . . .
>   make it a myth,
>   Then squeeze it
>   until the sea's blood dries on the grass
>   and the small fish walk on tails
>   to the sacred bazaar
>   to dance with unleavened loaves.
>
> Squeeze it until you,
>   O, Stranger,
>   ride home to the Sun's Center
>   and lose your unknown name
>   in the golden fire.
>   (maiz 1978, 36–37)

By so doing you acknowledge—even proclaim—your suffering and your pain. You break the conspiracy of silence about family violence. You do not do this to wallow in your pain but to choose, demand, and proclaim a better life for yourself—the life you deserve because you are a person of value. When you articulate your pain in this way, it can be joined to all aspects of your life. Then the suffering you experienced becomes the basis for a new understanding of yourself.

This proclamation of your pain can take the form of private or group therapy where you acknowledge the reality of your experience and work to resolve its negative impact on your life. It may involve sharing your history with carefully chosen friends and associates. It may even involve public proclamations. When appearing on radio and TV programs about family violence, I have often been asked to bring a survivor to share his or her personal story. Initially I was hesitant to ask anyone to make such a public, even though anonymous, statement. However, repeatedly survivors have said participation in such a program was a healing and empowering experience. It gave them a new sense of control over their abuse experience.

Such sharing confirms what Henri Nouwen describes when he says, "Community arises where the sharing of pain takes place, not as a stifling form of self-complaint, but as a recognition of God's saving promises. . . .[A] healing community [is formed] not because wounds are cured and pains are alleviated, but because wounds and pains become openings or occasions for a new vision . . . [And we discover] the living truth that the wound, which causes us to suffer now, will be revealed to us later as the place where God intimated his new creation" (1972, 96, 98).

Suffering Is Not Glorious

To accept and articulate your pain is not to glorify suffering. As a survivor of family violence you have suffered terribly for many years. Pain and fear were constants in your life, even from the innocence of your infancy. Your home, rather than being a source for learning meaning and purpose, was a source of pain and fear that raised questions: "Why is this happening to me? What have I done to deserve this? Why does God allow this? Why me?!" The failure to find satisfactory answers may have produced a crisis of faith.

The fact of suffering in the world has caused crises of faith for people from time immemorial. For Christians this conflict is frequently resolved by referring to the example of Jesus' sacrificial death. The example of Jesus, the suffering servant who "learned obedience through what he suffered" (Heb. 5:8) and who "humbled himself and became obedient to the point of death, even death on a cross" (Phil. 2:8), is often the object of reflection and meditation. His example is presented as a strong image that can give meaning, purpose, and dignity to one's personal suffering.

Jesus, the suffering servant, may have been held up to you as a model for the suffering you experienced in your family. John Calvin's admonition to a battered woman is well-known among religious persons working in the domestic violence field. Although Calvin had "special sympathy for women who are evilly and roughly treated by their husbands," he could not find himself "permitted by the Word of God, . . . to advise a woman to leave her husband." Instead he exhorted her to "bear with patience the cross which God has seen fit to place upon her; and meanwhile not to deviate from the duty which she has before God to please her husband, but to be faithful whatever happens" (quoted in Bussert 1986, 12).

Such an admonition advises submission to pain, not solidarity with it. Such advice not only fails to be helpful; it can also be dangerous. Research on family violence indicates that patient suffering does not lessen the level or frequency of violence. Often the violence merely escalates as the abuser seeks more control and further evidence of domination over the victim. Such advice glorifies and justifies suffering as an end in itself without questioning the content of one's faithfulness. Insights and strength can be achieved because one has been faithful to values that exist beyond the pain. Those values must express a choice for life in all its fullness (see Deut. 30:19), not a choice for violence and possible death. What value is being realized by this suffering? Who is being redeemed by it? Whose salvation is being accomplished?

Certainly not the batterer. If he is going to change his behavior, he must be confronted by a demand to stop his violence, and not be allowed to continue it unchallenged. He must be called to repentance, not confirmed in his violence by silence and acquiescence. As Sheila Collins points out in her book, *A Different Heaven and Earth,* invoking the suffering servant role model has too long "allowed men to escape from the responsibility of bearing their own burdens and coming to terms with their own sin and guilt. . . [it has] functioned to perpetuate that very dichotomy and alienation between human beings that the tradition claims to overcome" (1974, 88–89). Marie Fortune maintains that accountability is an essential part of the justice making necessary in violent families. This means confronting abusers and dignifying them by making them pay for the evil they commit. Anything less is to treat them as less than persons (1989, 117).

If you were a child in a family where there was spouse abuse, you were not redeemed by seeing the violence continue or by having your parents keep the family together "for the sake of the children." Lenore Walker reports that, in families where there is violence between spouses, the children often have emotional and educational problems and frequently are targets of abuse by the violent parent (1979, 30). The Children's Defense Fund reports that "it is estimated that about 40 percent of the children of victims of spousal abuse are also abused" (1988, 7). That is hardly a redemptive experience.

As a battered wife or an abused child you were not being redeemed by being victimized. One person may voluntarily place oneself in a position that results in suffering for a higher good. But abuse in one's family does not serve any noble purpose. As Marie Fortune states bluntly, such abuse "is not chosen and serves no greater good" (1983, 197).

You did not need to stay in an abusive relationship to learn greater patience. You had already suffered patiently for years before you came forward for assistance. You did not need more suffering to "build your character." Your character had already been formed by years of violence. To suggest that your abuse was a punishment for some past sin—besides being bad theology— reinforced the low self-image with which you were already struggling.

The Hebrew Bible's Book of Job confronts this false theology. Job, who "was blameless and upright, one who feared God and turned away from evil" (1:1) lost his wealth, his family, and has been inflicted with "loathsome sores . . . from the sole of his foot to the crown of his head" (2:7). He has become "a laughingstock to [his] friends" (12:4). Three of Job's "friends" come to console him. They turn out to be "miserable comforters" (16:2) because they spend most of their time challenging Job to admit the sinfulness that must be the reason for his suffering. Job debates his friends' accusations, saying, "I hold fast my righteousness, and will not let it go; my heart does not reproach me for any of my days" (27:6). As his suffering continues, Job complains of God's treatment of him. Finally, the Lord answers Job "out of the

whirlwind" (38:1) challenging "counsel by words without knowledge" (38:2) and demanding to know where Job and his friends
were when "I laid the foundation of the earth" (38:4). Although
God's answer to Job's complaints is basically, "My ways are not
your ways" (not always a satisfying answer when one is suffering), God does make it clear Job's suffering is not because of
anything he did wrong. In fact, God restores Job's health, family,
and fortunes when he prays that his "miserable comforters" not
be punished by God for the folly of their advice—for their
opinions that Job's suffering was the result of his sins.

Jesus' disciples were concerned about the same issue when they
asked whether a man's blindness was the result of his sin or that
of his parents. Jesus answered, "Neither this man nor his parents
sinned; he was born blind so that God's works might be revealed
in him. We must work the works of him who sent me . . ." (John
9:3–4). Suffering is not the sign of a moral flaw in one who
suffers, but it may constitute a moral flaw for those who do not
respond. All who observe suffering are challenged to "work the
works" of God, to respond with care and compassion and healing.
To do less is to give power to suffering, to accord it value that it
does not possess on its own.

Suffering does not have any inherent value—things are not good
and, therefore, to be passively accepted just because they are
painful. There is much pain in the world; even efforts for good
involve pain. Seeking physical fitness may result in painful stiffness;
raising children may produce stress; working for justice and peace
has been known to result in persecution. Pain is part of the
process—something that must be put up with—but the suffering
does not have an independent value. It is part of the reality of
seeking to improve an imperfect world, to "work the work" of God,
whether that means toning a flabby body, guiding the volatility of
puberty-stricken teenagers, or curbing the greed that produces
maldistribution of power and resources.

As a survivor, your world involved imperfect, abusive parents
or a domineering, assaultive spouse. They were not something
you deserved or sought and when the opportunities arose you did
not passively accept them; but they were (and in many ways still
are) a part of your life that must be acknowledged, confronted,
worked through, and overcome. "At issue is not what [you]
choose to endure or accept but what [you] refuse to relinquish.

Redemption happens when people refuse to relinquish respect and concern for others, when people refuse to relinquish fullness of feeling, when people refuse to give up seeing, experiencing, and being connected and affected by all of life" (Brown and Bohn, 19). Your redemption occurred when you survived, when you refused to be conquered by violence. Every time you confront your memories, every time you challenge the dysfunctions you learned, you "work the work" of your redemption.

As a victim of family violence, it is not enough to be told to "bear your cross." Even Jesus' suffering and death on the cross were not redemptive because they were painful. They were not isolated events or something he submitted to for the sake of the pain. Jesus did not want to undergo his suffering and death—he made that very clear in the Garden of Gethsemane when he prayed, "Father, if you are willing, remove this cup from me" (Luke 22:42). God did not make Jesus' suffering happen; God allowed those in authority to use their free will to pursue the preservation of their power. Jesus' suffering happened because he challenged the system of his time and because he refused to compromise in his commitment to truth and justice, love and liberation. In Gethsemane he chose not to run from the reality that resulted from his teachings, he refused to relinquish his mission, he chose to confront his accusers even if that might result in pain and death. Jesus' death was redemptive because it was a sign of his commitment to the real meaning of life, not because he had a masochistic affinity to suffering.

In the Christian account of Jesus' death we have a bonus. Its redemptive value is made manifest through his resurrection. If Jesus had merely suffered and died, his violent death would have had no evident redemptive outcome. His resurrection proclaimed the meaning, promise, and result of his suffering. Jesus' resurrection is not merely tacked on to the story to give it a happy ending. It was the result of the strength of Jesus' continuing commitment to his mission to new life that even death could not overcome. Jesus' resurrection proclaims that pain and suffering and death need not be controlling factors in our lives, but that they can and must be challenged and overcome. A "theology of the cross" that fails to include the resurrection advocates a theology of death without the promise of new life. All too often, you, as an abuse victim, were admonished to accept a theology of the cross that did not promise you new life and certainly not abundant life (see John 10:10).

The Christian proclamation of the power of Jesus' resurrection is a message that can guide the lives of persons who have suffered abuse. The power of Jesus' faith enabled him to face his total vulnerability and terrible suffering at the hands of those abusing power in his time, and it also enabled him to overcome death. That same message offers the possibility for new life to victims— the power to move beyond being a victim to the new life of a survivor. The resurrecting powers of healing and wholeness are available even for those who suffer the degradation of abuse from those they love.

The Christian churches also have as part of their tradition the exemplary wife and mother of the Gospels, who once proclaimed that the powerful should be "brought down" and the lowly "lifted up" (Luke 1:52–53). They have Jesus, who began his public ministry by announcing "release to the captives" and freedom for the oppressed (Luke 4:18) and who regularly reminded his followers that those in power should be servants (Luke 22: 24–27). The Gospels do not encourage violence and oppression and they do not exalt suffering as an end in itself. Violence, oppression, and suffering are to be eradicated; they are not virtues to be promoted. The good news of the Gospel is that God does not intend suffering: there is strength to overcome it and hope for liberation from oppression. This is the Christian message for victims and survivors alike—freedom from violence in your family and the power to overcome its spiritual devastation.

The Jewish tradition also has a rich heritage of redemptive promise for persons confronting family violence. Just as Jesus' death and resurrection is the primary faith-forming event for Christians, the exodus is the parallel event for Jews. Jews, however, have an advantage. There is no talmudic or rabbinic tradition that glorifies the period of slavery in Egypt as some Christian theology has exalted Jesus' suffering and death. For Jews the reality of the period of slavery is acknowledged, the pain and anguish are decried, but the focus of faith is on God's redemptive act of freeing the people. The focus of God's will and work are seen to be God's challenge to subjection and suffering. Just as the God of Abraham, Isaac, and Jacob saw fit to free the Israelite nation from the suffering and oppression of slavery, that same

God proclaims liberation for those bound by the terrors of violence in their families. That same liberating God announces the possibility of freedom to those presently enslaved by abuse. That same experience of freedom from enslavement can empower survivors to become new people who are formed and strengthened by suffering in intimate relationships—not a desirable way to be formed but a reality and a learning experience nonetheless—and who provide new understandings of personal and spiritual growth and of human relationships for all the world to learn.

The Jewish and Christian traditions' primary spiritual images contain insights that provide new light for persons who have suffered from family violence. The faith instilling and faith defining experiences of the exodus and the resurrection can take on new meaning for all modern day believers when considered in the light of the suffering and struggle of those held captive and threatened with death by the spiritual oppression of family violence. The Judeo-Christian message contains a "liberation theology" for survivors of family violence.

The liberating power of the exodus and the resurrection can be part of your experience as a survivor. Those events in Jewish and Christian history did not erase what had gone before—degrading slavery and violent death. Both the apostles and the Hebrew nation had to struggle to understand and integrate the power of those events for their lives—both groups had their periods of doubt and failure and both groups had to spend significant periods of time making their experience a meaningful part of their lives. During their time in the desert, the Hebrews even had to deal with some giants who made them feel like grasshoppers (Num. 13:32–33). Eventually both groups moved beyond their previously frightening, limiting, and devastating experiences to new land and new life. The people affected—Moses and the Israelite nation, and Jesus and his disciples—were called to community and to courage. You too have that same call!

Certainly the violence in your family was devastating and had a deadening effect on your life. It created gigantic anxiety and fear that stifled much that was creative and positive in your soul. Ignoring such devastation cripples not only those who suffer the violence but also society as a whole. Unmasking the illusion of familial bliss can be a profound spiritual experience for victims, survivors, and the community as a whole. Naming this senseless reality and proclaiming solidarity with the pain it has imposed will not lessen the pain of the victims, but it can offer a vision of another reality, and it can provide survivors with the strength to forgive and all persons with the opportunity to love. The virtues of love and forgiveness are, as Rabbi Harold Kushner has said, "the weapons God has given us to enable us to live fully, bravely, and meaningfully in this less-than-perfect world" (1981, 148). This is the principal challenge, the principal act of faith required of all people of God.

One of your important tasks as a survivor is to work your way through the maze filled with the dead ends of denial, self-blame, and victimhood created by your violent home. Such blocks are common to the abuse experience. But when you achieve full recognition of your abuse reality, when you lay the blame where it belongs, and when you proclaim that you are a worthwhile person who deserves better, then you have achieved solidarity with your pain, you have confronted your suffering, and you are well on the way to a faith in or trust of yourself and your potential for growth. As one survivor put it very graphically, "I now realize that I lived in shit, but *I* am *not* shit!"

Once you have achieved that realization, you can begin to trust your own anguish as a call for new direction in your life. That trust can enable you to celebrate your dignity and self-worth. It can enable you to fulfill the prerequisite for Jesus' second great commandment—you will love yourself so you can love "your neighbor as yourself" (Luke 10:27). You will be reconciled to yourself, freed from self-hate and enabled to feel compassion for yourself and others. Then you can recognize and trust a caring God. Such trust can heal; it can cast out fear.

When trust and respect for yourself are achieved, you also achieve the inner quiet necessary to convert the loneliness and isolation, which dominated your life as a victim, into solitude and inner peace. Then you can hear the questions of your life through the din of your anxieties, you can acknowledge your pain, you can let go of the negative images imposed by your abusers and you can be liberated from those images rather than being controlled by them. You can be released from fear of your abusers and freed to move on with your life.

6 | Tough Forgiveness

The ability to move forward with one's life in spite of anger and fear is critical to spiritual growth. Henri Nouwen describes the second movement of the spiritual life as "a painful search for a hospitable place where life can be lived without fear and where community can be found" (1975, 46). For you, this search has gone on for years. It was forced upon you within the confines of your home—the place to which one normally turns for hospitality. Therefore, you may carry within you deep hostility— often directed toward your parents or spouse. For you, to be able to receive others fully in hospitality you must learn to forgive your abusers. This is not an easy task, and it is one that many people, including therapists, say is unnecessary and even harmful for survivors.

Nouwen considers forgiveness a critical aspect in the second step of growth in the spiritual life, which is the movement from hostility to hospitality. It is also, however, the most misunderstood and often misused and abused part of the healing process. We will begin by determining what it is *not* (a critical part of knowing what it is), then try to comprehend the paradoxical connections between love, anger, and forgiveness, and end by examining the relationship between forgiveness and reconciliation. As important as forgiveness may be for spiritual growth, we must also remember the words of the prophet Jeremiah when he condemned those who "treated the wound of my people carelessly, saying, 'Peace, peace,' when there is no peace" (6:14).

The following incident illustrates the depth of this problem. As members of a new Grown-Up Abused Children group were settling in their places, one woman, Linda, broke in before I could call the group to order: "I have a question before we start." She demanded, "Are you going to tell me I have to forgive my mother for what she did? If you are going to tell me to forgive and forget, I'm not staying."

The theological and spiritual issue of forgiveness had never been put to me quite so bluntly. "No," I replied, after some quick reflection, "I am not going to tell you to forgive your mother. My first concern is that you get in touch with what happened to you as a child and with how you feel about that. I am certain one of your major feelings will be anger and that is very appropriate. As you determine what you want to do about that anger you may want to confront your mother. She may apologize and ask for forgiveness. Then you will have to decide whether you want to forgive her. I am certainly not going to encourage you to forgive and forget. I want you to remember what happened to you and how you feel about that. Then and only then, can you decide about forgiveness." "I can accept that," Linda said, settling back in her chair. "I'll stay."

Linda participated in the group for several months. During that time, she discussed her feelings toward her mother at great length. She had some angry, simulated conversations with her mother, but she never had the opportunity to actually confront her about the abuse. However, as Linda dealt with her feelings about her past, she became more gentle in her attitudes toward her mother. We never discussed the issue in theological terms again, but Linda seemed to develop an attitude of forgiveness toward her mother. She experienced greater peace concerning their relationship.

Was Linda correct in saying she did not want to forgive her mother? Was her attitude spiritually and psychologically unhealthy? Alice Miller, the well-known psychotherapist, abuse survivor, and advocate for survivors and children, maintains it is not. She writes, "It was my experience that it was precisely the opposite of forgiveness—namely, rebellion against mistreatment suffered, the recognition and condemnation of my parents' destructive opinions and actions, and the articulation of my own needs—that ultimately freed me from the past . . . . Forgiving has negative consequences, not only for the individual, but for society at large, because it means disguising destructive opinions and attitudes and involves drawing a curtain across reality so that we cannot see what is taking place behind it" (1991, 134, 136). As a survivor friend of mine put it very succinctly, "I need my anger. It keeps me clear about what was done to me and what I need to work on."

Forgiveness Is Not Forgetting

What, then, about the religious and spiritual problems supposedly involved in anger and hatred? What about all the admonitions you have received about forgiveness? Often, the first thing you may have been told by secular as well as spiritual counselors is "forgive and forget." You may have been reminded that God forgives us our many offenses, that Jesus said we should forgive "seventy-seven times" (Matt. 18:22) and that on the cross Jesus forgave his executioners "for they do not know what they are doing" (Luke 23:34).

Such admonitions may ring hollow and insensitive to you who have forgiven your assaultive husbands the allotted seventy-seven times—only to be beaten again. This forgiveness seems totally out of touch with reality for you who deeply love and desperately want to forgive your abusive parents and establish a safe, caring relationship but are constantly rebuffed. You may dream of living in a loving family where the pains of the past can be forgiven, but when the problems of the past are discussed, your parents deny them and say the problems are exaggerated or declare that you "only got what you deserved."

In your abusive family, forgiveness that forgot would have been an empty, even a dangerous virtue. Such forgiveness would have put you back into the very environment that caused you harm. It would have recreated the circumstances that allowed your offender to abuse you. To practice such forgiveness was dangerous business.

Even if you have moved away from your abusive parents or have separated from your abusive husband and are no longer in danger of further violence, to combine forgiving and forgetting is to deny the reality of the violence and injustice that has been done to you. To consider forgetfulness a desirable goal is to fail to recognize your dignity as a person.

Such an approach to forgiveness is insensitive to the depth of the harm and pain inflicted and is much too simple a solution to the realities of abuse. It also is not consistent with the religious notion of forgiveness. It denies the demanding, complex, and dialogic nature of the scriptural notion of forgiveness. As theologian Alan Richardson tells us: "Forgiveness is throughout conditional upon repentance, a word which quite clearly in its OT [Old Testament] and NT [New Testament] equivalents involves a change of mind and intention" (1950, 86).

Forgiveness that takes repentance seriously involves confronting the awful reality of what has been done. Children have been abused. Wives have been battered. Relationships have been shattered. Forgiveness in such circumstances demands that the harsh realities of pain, hurt, and violence—both physical and psychological—be taken seriously. It does not allow denying what happened or turning an offense into a nonoffense. Rather it means saying clearly, "What you did was wrong. That hurt me. But if you are willing to change, to really do things differently, I will forgive you."

Such an approach is also consistent with the biblical notion of repentance, which demands a complete change of life, a total reorientation in the way one lives. " 'Repent' in its NT usage implies much more than a mere 'change of mind'; it involves a whole re-orientation of the personality, a 'conversion' " (Richardson 1950, 192). In the case of a violent parent or spouse, this means they must admit they have been abusive (something that many never do), and they must get outside help to stop their battering behavior. Outside help is essential because research indicates it is virtually impossible for abusive parents or spouses to break the cycle of violence without professional intervention (see Walker 1979, 28–29). Thus, the acceptance of such assistance is an essential part of the act of repentance. It is a part of the reorientation of personality necessary for true conversion. Without it, there is no repentance and there can be no forgiveness in the biblical sense of the term.

This does not mean that you, the survivor, do not love your abuser and are not willing to forgive, nor does it mean that you bear a continuous grudge or festering anger. Even without your abuser's repentance, you can develop an attitude of forgiveness. You can acknowledge the validity of your anger and then "let it go," so you can move on with your life. You may admit the humanness of your batterer and even recognize the experiences in his or her life that contributed to the abusive behavior, but if he or she is unwilling to repent, to accept responsibility, to modify behavior, and to change his or her life, you are not able to complete the dialogue of forgiveness. You certainly should not forget what your abuser has done—that could be extremely dangerous. Some people are so prone to violence that to expose yourself to them is to invite abuse. They are better avoided.

You may be more than willing to follow Jesus' admonition, "If another disciple sins, you must rebuke the offender, and if there is repentance, you must forgive" (Luke 17:3). However, you may also be confronted with the reality, which Jesus acknowledged, that the offender may not repent: "If another member of the church sins against you, go and point out the fault when the two of you are alone. . . . But if you are not listened to, take one or two others along with you, so that every word may be confirmed by the evidence of two or three witnesses. If the member refuses to listen to them, tell it to the church; and if the offender refuses to listen even to the church, let such a one be to you as a Gentile and a tax collector" (Matt. 18:15–17).

As important as forgiveness is, repentance is equally critical. The Jewish tradition highlights this. "The idea of repentance is regarded as the brightest gem among the teachings of Judaism. Man would be the most unfortunate creature if he had no way of escape from sin. . . . According to talmudic-midrashic statements, repentance is of paramount importance to the existence of the world. It brings healing to the world" (Birnbaum 1967, 36–37). The responsibility for healing your abuse experience does not belong merely to you, the survivor, it also belongs to your abuser.

However, if you are confronted with an unrepentant abuser—and, unfortunately, many of you are—you are faced with resolving your anger and hurt without the prospect of full reconciliation. You are consigned the task of developing an attitude of forgiveness without the help of the dialogue that can result in reconciliation. You have to struggle to determine the appropriateness of your feelings without any admission of guilt on the part of your offender. You are required to struggle alone to comprehend experiences that defy comprehension. You must give perspective and order to events that were inherently chaotic and irrational.

With these pressures working against you, how are you to resolve your anger and express forgiveness? How are you to move toward hospitality? If full forgiveness and reconciliation are not possibilities, what are you to do? How can you move beyond your frustration, resentment, and pain? How can you let go of your anger, develop an attitude of forgiveness, and open yourself to the possibility of reconciliation when the option of fulfillment is not available?

As important as it may be for your healing and wholeness that you resolve your anger (which does not mean giving up your anger and the clarity it provides) and open yourself to forgiveness, they are not the first responses you should expect of yourself. Developing the attitude of forgiveness is a process that will differ in intensity and duration, depending on your personality and the extent and timing of your abuse. It is a complex and highly personal process that does not follow a time schedule. To expect to attain a highly refined level of insight and objectivity in a short time is unrealistic at best and spiritually debilitating at worst.

Developing an attitude of forgiveness is not an act of the will accomplished at a specific moment, but rather a series of steps, a complex process that involves several stages. Sidney and Suzanne Simon have identified six stages in what they call "forgiveness work." They are: denial, self-blame, victim, indignation, survivor, and integration. These stages often overlap, are not necessarily consecutive or linear, and can take several years (1990).

We have already discussed the Simons' first three stages as the beginning of spiritual growth. Naming your abuse, recognizing who was responsible for your suffering, and learning to feel good about yourself in spite of your history is part of achieving solidarity with your pain, and it is the beginning of affirming your worth as a child of God. Once you really know what persons who were supposed to love you did to you—and you believe you are someone who does not deserve such treatment—you finally have something to forgive! Before this realization, you felt what was done was not important or that it was your fault—so there was nothing to forgive. Now you know better and you are damn mad!

The Simons are clear about the importance of anger, "indignation," as part of the healing process of forgiveness. Anger and forgiveness are intimately connected with one another. They are part of an integrated process. Forgiveness cannot be achieved without accepting and affirming anger. But is this acceptable in religious circles? Will it help or hinder your spiritual development? I believe anger is essential to spiritual growth.

Anger Is a Virtue

To claim that anger is a virtue probably conflicts with much of what you learned in your family and in your church or synagogue. In your family when someone was angry someone else got hurt. Anger always became rage and resulted in violence or abuse. On the other hand, you may have had many good reasons to be angry. You were repeatedly abused and beaten. You were ridiculed and belittled. Your worth and dignity were severely maligned. If you dared to express any displeasure at what was happening to you, you were told your feelings were wrong. You were told to "shut up and be quiet." You may well have experienced further violence. In your family anger was hurtful or it was responded to with punishment.

As you have worked to reassert your value and affirm your life goals, you have probably discovered deep reservoirs of anger about the ways you were treated and the opportunities you were denied. As natural as anger might seem under the circumstances, you still remember that what you learned in your family and in your religious teachings told you anger was wrong. How often have you been told by religious leaders, "Don't be angry"? You were even told, "Don't feel angry." To do so is "wrong"; it's "sinful."

It is not hard to find religious admonitions against anger. The Hebrew and Christian Scriptures are filled with them.

> One who is quick-tempered acts foolishly,
> and the schemer is hated.
> (Prov. 14:17)

> Whoever is slow to anger has great understanding,
> but one who has a hasty temper exalts folly.
> (Prov. 14:29)

> One who is slow to anger is better than the mighty,
> and one whose temper is controlled than one who captures a
> city.
> (Prov. 16:32)

Those with good sense are slow to anger,
and it is their glory to overlook an offense.
(Prov. 19:11)

Do not be quick to anger,
for anger lodges in the bosom of fools.
(Eccles. 7:9)

Jesus puts his own special emphasis on the issue of anger when he says, "I say to you that if you are angry with a brother or sister, you will be liable to judgment" (Matt. 5:22).

At face value those scripture passages seem to confirm that anger is an evil emotion. However, if we read them more closely we recognize that the quotes from Proverbs and Ecclesiastes are not condemning all anger but only hasty anger. They are saying be slow to anger. Do not do it without careful consideration and "good sense." This is very different from never being or feeling angry.

On the other hand, Jesus' statement seems considerably more definitive. He seems to be attaching eternal damnation to anger. However, if we look at the Greek text, we discover that Jesus is not condemning all anger. Andrew Lester points out that the verb translated "are angry" is a present participle and is better translated "are *continuously* angry" or "*keeps on being* angry" (1983, 45; emphasis in original). Therefore, Jesus is condemning those who harbor anger, those who allow it to fester in their hearts, permeating their lives and relationships.

Paul in the letter to the Ephesians gives more specific advice concerning anger. When challenging the Ephesian Christians to live up to the fullness of their calling, he says, "Be angry but do not sin; do not let the sun go down on your anger" (4:26). He recognizes the prevalence and even the value of anger, but says it must not rule one's life.

Of course, that is easy advice to give. When one is sitting quietly at a desk writing, it is easy to say, "Be rational about your anger. Be angry, but not too much. Be angry, but turn the emotion off as soon as the incident is over and be open to reconciliation." It is good advice, but not always easy to follow. Anger, by its nature, is not purely rational. It can be volatile and abusive; it can be violent and destructive; it can turn to rage. In your home such anger and rage was the source of much of your pain.

Anger is an emotion and it generates a physiological reaction; adrenaline starts flowing. When people "get upset" and the adrenaline starts racing through their veins, they do not always feel rational. When we reflect on our own anger, we can identify with another of Paul's statements, "I do not understand my own actions. For I do not do what I want, but I do the very thing I hate. . . . I do not do the good I want, but the evil I do not want is what I do" (Rom. 7:15, 19). That was also the message often heard from parents and spouses—they didn't "know what came over" them. They didn't mean to hurt you.

If that is the case, wouldn't we all be better off if we simply avoided anger? It can be such a troublesome emotion. It so easily gets out of control and turns to rage. You who have lived in abusive families know better than most people how troublesome and even destructive anger can be. You may have tried to express the anger you felt at your treatment and suffered further rejection or violence as a result. You were told you were not supposed to be angry at your parents or your spouse. Your parents or spouse heaped more abuse on you because you attempted to express your feelings about your treatment. As a result you find it easier and safer to follow the standard religious admonition, "Don't be angry!"

As practical as that advice may seem, it usually does not work over the long run. My experience with survivors indicates that many of their present problems stem from repressed anger. For you it may be the source of unexplained tensions and anxieties and even some illnesses. Unresolved anger about your past may contribute to problems of drug or alcohol abuse or to irrational or excessive outbursts of rage. This anger may be directed at yourself or at persons or situations that do not merit such responses. Such misdirected anger may be causing you serious problems. It may be destroying relationships; it may even have resulted in lawsuits or criminal prosecution.

Social ethicist Beverly Wildung Harrison expressed this dilemma accurately when she wrote:

We need to recognize that where the evasion of feeling is widespread, anger does not go away or disappear. Rather, in interpersonal life it masks itself as boredom, ennui, low energy, or it expresses itself in passive-aggressive activity or in moralistic

self-righteousness and blaming. Anger denied subverts community. Anger expressed directly is a mode of taking the other
seriously, of caring. The important point is that where feeling is
evaded, where anger is hidden or goes unattended, masking itself,
there the power of love, the power to act, to deepen relation,
atrophies and dies (1985, 15).

Thus, trying to deny anger instead of acknowledging it and
dealing with the resultant feelings really means that you remain
angry. The anger continues past many sundowns and festers until
it breaks forth on a totally inappropriate day and strikes out at
someone who does not deserve it. Denial is not, therefore, a
good-sense approach to anger; in fact, it is the way of fools. The
way of "great understanding" is to acknowledge anger and to be
honest and explicit about it without harming others. This means
learning to recognize what hurts and upsets you, acknowledging
your right to be upset and learning and practicing direct, honest,
and nonabusive confrontation. This is not an easy task, even for
people who grew up in nonabusive homes, but it can be learned;
it can be done.

One of the Gospel passages that often makes religious persons
uncomfortable—and for which they search ways to explain
away—is the account of Jesus driving the merchants and money
changers from the Temple (Matt. 21:12–13; Mark 11:15–17; Luke
19:45–46; John 2:14–16). This story, apparently important to the
early Christians because it is reported by all four evangelists,
presents a Jesus who is very angry at what he sees being done in
the Temple. John's Gospel is very careful to make it clear why
Jesus got so angry: "Zeal for your house will consume me" (2:17).

This Gospel story contains an important lesson for survivors of
abuse. The lesson is that anger is a necessary and important
emotion. It can even be called a virtue because it is a measure of
what a person is zealous about. It would have been a failure on
Jesus' part if he had not gotten angry at the abuses he saw
happening in the Temple. He would have failed to be concerned
about the proper use of his "Father's house." His zeal and
commitment would have been lacking.

As victims of abuse, you had every right to be zealous in your
anger about what was being done to you. You were being
mistreated and abused. Your rights and dignity as a human being

were being undermined and attacked. That was and is something for which you have every right and even a responsibility to be angry. Anything less in yourself or in those who were aware of what was happening is a failure of zeal and commitment.

One of the most devastating things you may have experienced as an abuse victim was that often you were not allowed to be angry about the way you were being treated. The perpetrators told you that you were not supposed to be angry; you experienced more violence if you did express anger. Soon you learned that anger was not an effective response to what was being done to you; it was not safe. Ultimately, you came to believe that you were not worthy of anger, that there was nothing about you that merited such zeal.

You may have sought counseling and again may have been told not to be angry. In effect you were being told that you were not worth caring about, that your well-being did not merit zeal. This was not the message you needed to hear. You needed to have your anger accepted and even encouraged as an appropriate response to the injustice that had been done to you.

Unfortunately, you may have survived violence and yet not be in touch with your anger. You have had to repress it for so many years that you may have lost touch with the feeling. You do not even know what it feels like to be angry and may even be uncomfortable with the thought of being angry because you believe it is wrong.

Denial of anger may be particularly true for women who have been trained in "mandatory 'niceness' " (Wood 1988, 1). You have been so conditioned to be "nice girls," to be "sugar and spice and everything nice" that expressing anger has become virtually impossible.

The experience of one group member illustrates this. Carol had been a member of a Grown-Up Abused Children group for almost two years. Although she had made great progress, one problem persisted. Every time the topic of anger came up or someone in the group expressed anger in any way, she would push her chair away from the circle and cringe in fear. She almost curled up in a fetal position in her chair. Each time this would happen the group would ask her why she did it, why she was so afraid. She responded that when anyone got angry, she was afraid they were going to hit her. The group reassured her that no one was angry at her, no one was going to strike her. These reassurances had little effect.

One day her response broadened to include another fact. She said, "I am afraid I am going to get angry." She could offer no explanation about why someone else's anger was going make her angry.

One meeting, when Carol again retreated to her corner and curled up in her fetal position, I pulled my chair directly in front of her. Gently, I unwrapped her arms from around herself and encouraged her to put one of her clenched fists in the palm of my hand. She did so with great reluctance. I urged her to push on it. Her response was, "I can't. I might hurt you." I assured her that it would not hurt me. She would not be striking me but only pushing against my hand. I explained that I was trying to get her to release the tension that was coiled in her body. Reluctantly and hesitantly, she began to push on my hand, pausing periodically to inquire if she were hurting me. I assured her she was not. She finally relaxed a little but stated that she had to stop because she was afraid to do any more. We stopped and she rejoined the group.

This process was repeated periodically over the next several weeks. I got her to the point where she would punch gently at the palm of my hand. Finally, she got more aggressive with her punches, and I had to hold a chair cushion in my hand. Each time, we discussed her feelings about what she was doing, as well as her anger and the object of that anger.

After one such session Carol confided that she wished she had the courage to go into one of the porno shops a few blocks from the campus. Amazed, the group members asked why she wanted to do that. Her reply was, "I understand you can buy life-size, anatomically correct dolls. I would like to get one to beat on." A woman in the group chimed in, "What would you like, a male or female? I will sew one for you by the next meeting."

True to her word, the woman arrived at the next meeting with a life-sized stuffed doll. She had sewn a shirt to a pair of pants, added a head and stuffed the whole arrangement with old rags and packing material. And if you unzipped the jeans, Max—as he was quickly named—was anatomically correct.

Carol's initial reaction to Max was fear. Gradually, she approached him, propped up in a chair, and punched him gently, stepping back and laughing nervously each time she did it. Gradually her blows became more vigorous and she attacked Max with a vengeance. Soon he was out of the chair and on the floor and being kicked and punched repeatedly while Carol screamed obscenities. All the time she was doing this, I stood behind her with my hands gently on her shoulders saying, "Carol, remember who this is, remember who you are really angry at." Eventually Carol's anger subsided and she collapsed in a chair in exhaustion. She surveyed the group and asked if everyone was all right. They assured her they were fine and that what she had done was good.

Carol began to talk with greater clarity than ever before about the abuse her father had heaped upon her and the anger that she always felt but was afraid to express. Her anger had reached such proportions that she was afraid she would hurt someone if she ever let herself get angry. She was afraid she would never be able to stop if she allowed herself to be angry. This was the first time she ever allowed such feelings to surface.

"What do I do now?" she asked. "I feel relieved, but I am also afraid that I am going to get angry again. I won't have Max to beat on and I may hurt someone." I assured her that she would feel angry again and that she would be have to be careful to control it around other people. When she was alone, she might try beating on pillows or overstuffed chairs. We would need to have many more discussions in the future to help her learn to manage her anger and appropriately express it.

Carol's anger was a topic of discussion at each of the meetings over the next several weeks. In the beginning, she acknowledged that she felt angry on many occasions—"Almost constantly." Gradually, the frequency of the emotion diminished and she was able to put her feelings in perspective. She was able to sort out what things were appropriately making her angry and which events were simply reminding her of her father's abuse in the past. She developed additional methods for expressing her anger, including calm conversation with people who may have offended her. She developed a whole new repertoire of interpersonal skills.

Carol's story is one of the more dramatic examples of a grown-up abused child getting in touch with and learning to express her anger. It exemplifies some of the kinds of problems that you as a survivor may also have with anger. You may be afraid of other people's anger, you may get confused, anxious, and afraid about your own anger, and you may be afraid that your own emotions will overwhelm you. You also may have moral or religious conflicts about allowing yourself to feel angry.

As a survivor of abuse you are not alone in having difficulty dealing with anger. Such an inability to identify and express anger is not uncommon in our society, even for people who have not experienced abuse. Learning to express such new emotions can be a difficult and delicate process. Most people feel uncomfortable with it. Even counselors can be uncomfortable with other people's expressions of anger. I must confess to no little anxiety when Carol began to rant and rave at Max. It is not easy to sit quietly while someone throws a "temper tantrum." It is not easy to be supportive if some of the rage is inappropriately directed at you. The important thing to remember at this point is that anger is a legitimate and important virtue. It is, in fact, a measure of one's self-esteem and spiritual life, a gauge of one's values and commitments.

Anger as a Tool for Spiritual Growth

Even if we accept anger as a virtue (remember Paul did advise his Ephesian Christians to "be angry"), that does not mean anger should become a way of life. Righteous anger, anger properly directed at an injustice, is an appropriate response to abuse, but it should not become all-consuming. Although anger is a healthy response to victimization and an important part of the reaffirmation of your dignity, it must be managed with "great understanding" and "discretion"—a difficult task.

On a purely theoretical level, the question must be asked about the role of anger and its expression in good mental health. Is it an appropriate emotion? Should it be repressed and controlled, or should it be vented and expressed with great energy and conviction?

Few people would deny that anger is a part of everyone's life, although some grown-up abused children say that they have never experienced anger—their blocking survival mechanism was that effective. But is it more effective to keep it to yourself, or express it to the world around you? Will you feel better or worse after you express your anger? We have all probably had occasions when we felt better and others when we felt worse.

For purposes of this discussion, let me define anger as an emotional response to insult or injury and the communication of those feelings. That response is virtuous because it expresses your zeal. The emotional response may have attendant physiological reactions and there are many different ways that these feelings can be communicated. The feelings can be communicated to the source of injury or to others who will share the offended person's reaction.

What constitutes an insult or injury can vary greatly from person to person and between cultures and families. In some ethnic groups, loud arguments are the order of the day. If members of the family have not disagreed vigorously about some issue during a family reunion, it has not been a successful event. Such discussions in other families would be cause for insult, and the family members would never speak to each other again.

As a survivor of abuse you may have distorted images of what constitutes an insult or injury. You may, for example, be extremely sensitive to certain situations. Because of the way situations were handled in your family, statements intended to be helpful are seen as put-downs, gestures intended to comfort are perceived as threats. You may need help to reinterpret such experiences in your life.

Being told, "You should not be so sensitive" is not helpful. You need to see why your behaviors are out of the ordinary in order to determine what would be appropriate and to see that the situations you are reacting to are in a different social context from what you experienced in your family. What was an insult in your family was not necessarily so in other situations. A gesture of friendship for other people (for example, a hand extended to pat you on the back) may have been a threatening act in your family.

On the other hand, you may be totally insensitive to insult or injury. You accept any ridicule or put down as treatment you deserve. You see no reason to be angry, no matter what injustice is perpetrated on you. Such acts are merely a confirmation of your worthlessness. As we have seen, before you can consider anger a virtue, you must first be convinced of your self-worth. Then, you will be able to develop an appropriate sense of insult and injury.

When an injury is perceived, most people experience physiological reactions—muscle tension, clenched fists, flushed cheeks, sweaty palms. Research indicates that anger induces increased pulse rate and higher blood pressure. Such reactions are a natural part of the human response to threat or injury. Even survivors who deny they ever feel angry, do so through clenched teeth. For them, and maybe for you, the emotion of anger is too dangerous. If you responded with anger when you were abused, it caused greater violence. Instead of anger being a method for regaining control over your life, it resulted in more loss of control. Even outside your family anger may not have been safe: it may have resulted in actions that brought you grief rather than peace or respect. For you, anger may be mixed with fear, anxiety, and frustration. You have learned it is safer to repress and block your feelings. For you, denial is the best policy.

But is it the best policy? Research indicates that the repression of anger increases the physiological reactions. Repression contributes to high blood pressure and may result in damage to one's heart. A psychological adage maintains that depression is anger turned inward. Survivors of abuse frequently suffer from depression, sometimes severe, often low-grade, but chronic. Such evidence suggests that denial of anger is not a recommended course of action. It may be contributing to a depression which is unwittingly self-abusive.

However, if you learned to repress your feelings of anger, you may not realize you have anything to communicate. How do you get from denial to communication? You would do well to begin by observing your body language—your tension, your flushed face, your clenched fists. Do not ask yourself whether or not you are angry. Instead ask, "When such a thing happens, or when I recall what my parents did to me, how does my body feel? Do I feel tense in my shoulders, knots in my stomach, or hot all over? What does that physical feeling make me want to do?" Ask yourself what you would like to do to relieve those symptoms, if you were able to do anything you wanted.

This kind of reflection should help you identify your physiological reactions to injury or insult. After you have been able to identify your reactions, you can connect them to the emotion and realize that you are feeling angry. Then, you must remind yourself that anger is indeed an appropriate reaction, that it is natural and even virtuous to feel angry in such a situation, and that you have many different, effective, and spiritually healthy ways to deal with and express your anger.

What are those appropriate ways to express anger? Many people, not only those who have suffered family violence, feel that anger is a useless and even destructive emotion. It is better to keep it to yourself. It does not do any good to express anger; it often makes matters worse. Is there a way to express anger without making things worse?

The most popularly acclaimed method for expressing anger today is ventilation—letting it all hang out, getting things off your chest, yelling and screaming. This is touted as a cure for high blood pressure and a means to better mental health. It certainly was what Carol did, and it seemed to help.

For persons who have denied anger for many years, ventilation may be an effective way to get in touch with the emotion. It can help you learn what anger feels like and understand its process. You can also learn not to fear it. You can discover that, even in the throes of anger, you still have a level of control and you can regain complete control. If this ventilation is done in a controlled environment, one where you and others around you are protected and safe, ventilation can be a productive process. If a supportive environment is also available (that is, among people who can help you reflect on your experience and be clear about whom you are angry at and how your process of anger works) ventilation can become a fruitful learning experience.

But is it the best way to react? Some abuse survivors are abusers of others. They do not need to learn how to express anger. They do so violently on many occasions. Suzanne K. Steinmetz in her book, *The Cycle of Violence*, points out that the expression of violence (its ventilation) within families does not relieve tension and help the families deal with anger more creatively. It increases violence and teaches children that such behavior is acceptable (1977, 24). Her data is certainly not a strong endorsement of the ventilation/ catharsis approach to anger.

Persons who work with abusive males also maintain that for such men the violent expression of anger is addictive. The physiological reactions associated with anger and its violent expression produce a high that they find exhilarating. These persons do not need to discover how to express their anger; they must learn to control it. Their first task is to stop their violence.

However, some people repress their anger even while they are being violent. Some survivors, who were not normally violent or angry, report having committed acts of violence without having experienced anger in the process. They felt no emotion at all. It was almost as if they watched themselves perform the violent act. Some abusers also report having no emotional feelings during a battering episode. Their violence had no emotional content. Even though they were violent, they had successfully repressed their anger.

Such persons need to connect their anger with their violence. They need to recognize their anger in its early stages and identify the physiological responses that precede the violence. Then they can control it. They must learn that there are other ways to express what they are feeling. Ventilating their anger in controlled environments is helpful to them, but this is not learning to yell for the sake of yelling; it is learning to recognize anger so that the emotions connected to insult or injury can be properly expressed. Survivors of abuse need to recognize their emotions, then they can examine various ways to express them. Violence is certainly not appropriate and yelling and screaming are not the only alternatives. As Carol Tavris says, "Anger means that something in your life is wrong" (1982, 44). Once that fact is recognized, a person can begin to change what is wrong. Then anger can be used constructively.

Ventilation is not the only way to get in touch with one's anger. If you find it too threatening to get so animated, you might try drawing, painting, or writing to get in touch with your feelings. Whatever method you use, the important thing is to get in touch with what is wrong in your life so you can begin to change it. Augustine has written, "Hope has two beautiful daughters: anger and courage. Anger at the way things are and courage to see that things do not stay the way they are." Your anger can help you find the courage to change your life.

One way you may want to use your anger is to confront your parents about what they did to you. This task must be approached cautiously. You must be clear about what you hope to accomplish. Do you expect to get an apology and effect some change in your parent's behavior? That has proven to be unlikely. In most cases the parents of people who were abused years ago will deny the charges or say they are blowing things out of proportion. If that is your sole reason for undertaking the confrontation, you are probably better off not trying.

If you believe that, even if you do not receive an apology, you would feel better for having "said your piece," this can be constructive. It does not always have to be done directly to your parents. Some times it cannot be done because they are deceased or refuse to meet. In such cases, people have role-played conversations with their parents or written out what they wanted to say and then decided whether or not they needed to speak to them directly. One woman flew to New Jersey to say what she had to say at her father's grave. In such cases people find it helps to have communicated their feelings and articulated what was important to them. This helped them pinpoint what was of concern to them: "It was not that he hit me that was important, but what he said when he did it." "What really upset me is that my mother did not stop it."

This communication of feelings—whether on a piece of paper, in a soft, modulated voice, or through screamed obscenities while beating on a punching bag—can provide the catharsis necessary to help you stop internalizing the negative messages you received. You are finally able to place them outside yourself so that you can see that they are not the definition of who you are. You can then realize that what may be wrong with your life is not yourself, but persons and forces outside of yourself that you can choose to reject. Dr. Bernie Siegal, who guides people in spiritual methods for combating cancer, recommends that patients get angry with their disease because it moves them from fear of their disease into action, doing what they can do. Your anger confronts the fear created by your abuser and begins your rejection of false and negative messages about yourself and your life.

Prayer can also be a meaningful way to demonstrate your anger. You can express to God your anger about what was done to you. You can pray for vindication and just retribution. Although it may not be considered typical material for prayer, Psalms, the prayer book of the Bible, is filled with creative poetic expressions of desires for reprisal. There is a whole class of psalms known as the lamentation psalms. The authors of the psalms were not afraid to pray that those who had hurt them would be repaid "according to their work, and according to the evil of their deeds" (Ps. 28:4). They even suggested to God ways that this could be done: breaking their enemies' arms (Ps. 10:15), breaking "the teeth in their mouths" (Ps. 58:6), casting them "down into the lowest pit" (Ps. 55:23), making their children orphans (Ps. 109:9). Although God may not be inclined to take your advice and become a professional assassin, such psalmic expressions of your anger can become "a way for healing candor" because by articulating it in prayer, your anger can be "fully experienced, embraced, [and] acknowledged" (Brueggemann 1984, 123). Fantasies of your abusers becoming "like whirling dust, like chaff before the wind" (Ps. 83:13), like grass "that withers before it grows" (Ps. 129:6) can have a salutary, cleansing effect on the hostility that has been consuming your life. "While we may think [this motif is] ignoble and unworthy, it demonstrates that in these psalms . . . Israel does not purge this unguardedness but regards it as genuinely faithful communication" (Brueggemann 1984, 55). Such prayer can help focus your zealous anger and invoke God's help to change what is wrong in your life.

Even more than ridding yourself of old, negative messages your justifiable anger can also open your life to unknown or previously discounted possibilities. Susan's experience illustrates this aspect.

Max, Carol's life-sized dummy, had a short but useful life. Periodically he would be taken from the garbage bag, where he was stored behind a chair in my office, to receive the newly discovered anger of group members or individual clients. However, his stitching finally wore out and I had to substitute an old heavy-duty punching bag from the YMCA in the building where my office was located.

Susan had begun to remember her father's sexual abuse. She began to realize the source of her coolness toward and discomfort with her father. She asked if she might try expressing her anger on the punching bag in her next session. She came to the session a few minutes late. She had gone to the university gym to change from her office clothes to her running sweats. Thus attired, she was able physically to attack the bag without hesitation. Her physical and verbal attacks on the bag were similar to Carol's. After she regained her composure, we discussed her feelings and reactions.

The next week Susan was again a few minutes late and was dressed in her sweatsuit. I said, "I assume you don't feel you're done with the punching bag yet." "I'm not sure." she replied. "There's still something unfinished and I wanted to be prepared." I dragged the bag out from behind the chair and placed it in front of her. She sat looking at it for several minutes, again imaging it as her father. Finally, she looked up with tears in her eyes. "I have the strangest feeling," she said. "I want to hit this thing and I also want to hug it." "Go ahead and do whichever seems right and comfortable," I replied.

In turn Susan hit the bag and yelled her anger at her father and then hugged that same dusty, gray bag with the most tender embrace. She wept over the relationship she never had with her father. When she finished with the bag, she acknowledged that she never knew she had such feelings for her father. As long as she could remember their relationship had been one of distance and disdain. A whole new range of possibilities were opened to her.

Susan experienced in a very concrete and graphic way the intimate relationship between love and hate, between anger and caring. She experienced what it means to love someone while hating what they do. She discovered how the repression of one set of emotions also blocks others. She confronted one of the basic conflicts of life and spiritual growth—being open to the courage to build a hospitable community even in the face of one's pain and one's fears.

That task, the task of confronting the conflicts of life and finding the courage to grow in virtue, is a challenge that faces all persons who are serious about their spiritual life. The question of how one can be angry about evil done by one's neighbor (parent, spouse) and still love that neighbor (parent, spouse) is the essence of forgiveness of one's enemies and growing spiritually. The reconciliation of anger and forgiveness is the next phase of a healing spirituality.

Forgiveness Is Letting Go

If you can accept that anger is not something evil but is rather a measure of your zeal, an indication of what you care about and are committed to, then when you recognize your inherent value as a person, you are justifiably angry about what was done to you. You now care enough about yourself to be zealous for your own welfare. You now recognize that evil was done to you, a valued child of God. More than that,

you realize that you have earned the right to call yourself a survivor and to declare:

I am alive. I was hurt and what I did because I was hurt made a difference in my life. I do not deny it, but I did live through it, and I've learned from it.

I am okay. I now know that I was not responsible for the hurtful things other people did to me and that I do not have to go on beating myself over the head for the things for which I was not responsible.

I am back in the driver's seat. I may have been powerless at the time I was hurt, but I am not powerless now. I was victimized, but I am not a victim. I am an adult, and I can steer my life in the direction that I want it to go.

I am better than I've ever been. I am strong enough to face life without using indignation as a shield to protect me. I can feel angry, but I am not a slave to my anger (Simon, 171, emphasis theirs).

To deny your right as a survivor to be angry is not only to rob you of your dignity, but also to short-circuit your healing process and restrict your possibilities for growth. Zeal that generates anger is a necessary step in your healing process, but it is not the last one. It merely enables you to confront your abuse experience and identify it for what it is so you can finally let it go and attain inner peace. Marie Fortune quotes a survivor who attained such peace: "I will not let it continue to make me feel bad about myself. I will not let it limit my ability to love and trust others in my life. I will not let my memory of the experience continue to victimize and control me" (1983, 209).

This is the true religious meaning of forgiveness. When Jesus affirmed Peter's leadership, he said, "I will give you the keys of the kingdom of heaven, and whatever you bind on earth will be bound in heaven and whatever you loose on earth will be loosed in heaven" (Matt. 16:19). Jesus used the same language after his discussion of people who refuse to take correction for their offenses against members of the community (Matt. 18:18). When Jesus gave his disciples the power to forgive sins after his resurrection (John 20:21–23), he expressed this in terms of the power to forgive or to "retain" sins. Jesus was concerned about the need to free people from the oppression of failure—their own and others'. Creation spirituality theologian Matthew Fox has said, "Forgiveness is another word for letting go. . . . Forgiveness is about letting go of guilt—some imagined, some real—and about letting go of fear" (1983, 163). It is also about letting go of that part of anger that seeks vengeance and retaliation. It is about letting go of the guilt or shame you feel about the way you responded to your abuse or your abuser, and the regrets you have about the misdirections you may have taken in your healing process. In short, it is about going beyond a painful past to a promising future.

Lewis B. Smedes has said, "Forgiveness is God's invention for coming to terms with a world in which despite their best intentions people are unfair to each other and hurt each other deeply" (1986, 12). This invention allows us to live in solidarity with our pain but not be controlled by it—it extinguishes the power of the pain. "Forgiving is love's revolution against life's unfairness" (Smedes 1986, 126) that enables us to liberate ourselves from the "laws" of fairness and even scores. It is the power that enables us to offer a prayer for our abuser through teeth still clenched in anger—and eventually come to mean it. Such a response is not an easy one—neither was surviving your abuse—but you did the one and you can learn to do the other. It just takes time, patience, and practice.

Forgiveness that lets go does not condone the violence done. It does not forget it. It is simply the attitude in you, the victim now a survivor, that allows you to acknowledge your anger, appreciate your zeal, and internalize the new awareness of yourself that both have given you. You recognize the reality of your abusive past, but you also recognize that the experience is past. You have grown to know yourself as more than—and much beyond—your abusive past. As you move beyond your anger, you are no longer dominated by your abuser, your memories, or even your desire for retaliation. You are open to forgive your batterer if he or she ever comes to you in repentance.

Beyond Forgiveness to Reconciliation

That special moment when repentance and forgiveness unite in reconciliation may be a long time coming. It involves a long and complicated process for two parties. We have now reached the part of the forgiveness process that is dialogic. If you hope to attain true reconciliation, you must remember that it is a process that involves both parties. It is not enough for you, as a former battered woman or abused child, to be willing to forgive; your abuser must also be willing to repent. He must acknowledge his wrong and convert himself to a different life. The words for conversion in both the Hebrew and Christian scriptures mean "an actual turning around," a "radical change of direction" (Lechman 1988, 19). Only when the perpetrator does this are you, the survivor, called upon to consider the final step in the forgiveness process—reconciliation.

To reach this point, both parties must have done their own healing work separately; it cannot be accomplished through traditional family counseling that treats husbands and wives together as a single unit. The disparity in power in an abusive family is so profound that it is unrealistic to expect joint counseling to uncover the underlying conflicts within the relationship. This healing is not accomplished by a simple act of the will, such as taking Jesus as one's personal savior. Jesus did come to reconcile humans to God, but there are important human connections to that process. Jesus pointed out that there are concrete things one must do before claiming union with God: "So when you are offering your gift at the altar, if you remember that your brother or sister has something against you, leave your gift there before the altar and go; first be reconciled to your brother or sister, and then come and offer your gift" (Matt. 5:23–4).

This passage makes it very clear "that the making of reparations precedes offerings to God. Neighbor is the prerequisite for communion with God. . . . Reconciliation is a human act, done before approaching the throne. . . . The work of reconciliation is human work to be done by those who are guilty" (Brueggemann 1989, 34). Abusers must also involve themselves in the difficult and painful process of admitting their violence and changing their patterns of behavior. Reconciliation involves "a new creation" (2 Cor. 5:17), a radical transformation. We should expect nothing less in the process of reconciliation for family violence.

Reconciliation with one's converted abuser can be the ultimate challenge of hospitality for a survivor, but it can also bear the greatest promise. You can become part of a new creation, you can experience new or forgotten parts of who you are and who the abuser is. Just as Susan recovered forgotten feelings of affection for her father as she alternately hit and hugged the punching bag, you too may recover positive feelings for your abuser and remember forgotten kindnesses and good times. Such remembrance is critical to reconciliation because it helps us experience the whole of a relationship, the good (as small as it may be) as well as the bad.

You may also realize that the reconciliation process applies not only to your relations with others but also to your relations with yourself. You may also develop an attitude of forgiveness toward yourself, become reconciled with and within yourself. The abuse you experienced may have created hostility toward yourself. You may have learned negative images of yourself and acquired counterproductive behaviors. These images and response patterns may have caused you to do things with which you are not pleased. You learned distrust, suspicion, hostility, and violence. You may not have always acted in the most responsible manner. Your healing process may have involved false starts and backsliding, you may have been locked in negative behaviors for long periods of time, and you may have hurt or alienated others in the process. As you assess your process of growth, you may have to forgive yourself for whatever failures may have been your responsibility—and who of us does not have some failures? You must also recognize that you did the best you could under the circumstances, circumstances that were extremely negative and oppressive. You need to "let loose" your negative feelings so they do not run your life. Where you may have hurt others you, too, must repent and seek reconciliation in order to create a new reality.

Thus, reconciliation with your abuser is not the only work to be done in this phase of your healing. You must also become reconciled to yourself. You must harmonize the elements of your life: your dysfunctional behaviors with your productive skills, your frustration about the slow pace of your healing with the real progress you have made, your shame at what was done to you with your pride about your survival, your sorrow at your failings with your satisfying successes in the face of enormous odds. When you recognize that the pain and vulnerability you experienced as an abuse victim have taught you compassion and given you a commitment to justice, you will have moved from being an abuse survivor to an abuse thriver who is an advocate for all persons who suffer injustice. As you acknowledge the progress you have made, you will also recognize the work that still needs to be done. You will accept the ongoing challenge of human development.

All of this will help you put your abuse experience in perspective—in the Simons' term, "integrate" it into your life. Just as you recognize your abuser as more than an abuser, you see yourself as more than a survivor of abuse. You are also a mother, a friend, a good cook, and an athlete. As hard as it may be to imagine now, you will also come to realize what you gained from the abuse experience—insights into people, instincts for survival, sensitivity to people's moods. You will realize that the abuse that was a curse in your life has provided you with some blessings. Ellen Bass has said that when survivors heal, "They become people who have thoroughly explored themselves; their strengths and their weaknesses, their hopes and their fears, their values, their commitments. Although they carry scars, many are healthier than people who never were abused, who never had reason to explore themselves so intimately and know themselves so well" (in Lew 1990, xxii). Abuse was no doubt "a hell of a way" to learn such things, but you did learn them. As one of the Simons' clients told them: "Going through hell really does have its benefits" (1990, 209).

Hell is the ultimate religious image for hostility. Going through hell is an appropriate description for what you experienced as a victim of abuse. As a survivor of family violence, you have faced the most devastating form of hostility. As you have resisted the effects of that hostility, healed your wounds, conquered your fear, and grown in love, you have proceeded through the second stage of spiritual development. Your hope has begun to produce a new reality. You have overcome distrust and fear and created community.

7 | Unmasking Our Illusions About God

Having come this far in your healing and spiritual growth process, you may be in an excellent position to complete the next step in your spiritual journey. Concerning this step Henri Nouwen says, "It is only in the lasting effort to unmask the illusions of our existence that a real spiritual life is possible. . . [W]e need the willingness and courage to reach out far beyond the limitations of our fragile and finite existence toward our loving God in whom all life is anchored" (1975, 80).

As a survivor, you are well aware of "the limitations of our fragile and finite existence"—you have confronted them on a daily basis. You know the precariousness of existence because you have lived in dangerous and even life-threatening environments. You have learned that life is not fair and that there are no guarantees. You have experienced vulnerability and faced death; you have looked over the edge of nothingness. Few human illusions of power and control have survived your abusive experiences.

You may be willing and eager to turn noisy loneliness into peaceful solitude and change raging hostility to forgiving hospitality, but you may be less anxious to reach out to a God who is frequently identified as a caring father. This image may raise problems for you. Since your experience of a father or parent as one who should have cared for you was not positive, it may not be clear to whom you are relating.

Who Wants a Fatherly God?

You may find it difficult to get very excited about belief in a God who is addressed as "Father." You may not be able to respond to such a concept because the notion of fatherhood generates feelings of revulsion not respect, anger not attraction, and anxiety rather than enthusiasm. Since the concept of the fatherhood of God seems integral to the Jewish and Christian traditions, you are confronted with a profound problem of belief and of spirituality.

The description of God as Father may severely limit your ability to believe in God. If a key element of divinity is fatherhood, you lack experience with which to relate to that concept. Without the experience of having had a caring parent or loving father, you may not be able to conceive of a supreme caring Parent or loving Father whom you might honor or turn to in times of need.

This problem is not limited to those who experienced abuse from their fathers. Despite the fact that the Judeo-Christian tradition has generally used masculine images for God and has ignored the feminine images that put God in the role of a loving mother, merely correcting this distortion will not solve this problem. In reality you were not safe in your home. Whichever parent may have been abusive, the other was not protective and caring or was too weak and ineffectual to correct the abusive situation. Your basic experience was fear and danger in that place which ought to have been safe and comforting. Whatever the gender of your abuser, you do not have adequate experience to understand the concept of a parental figure who cares for and protects you. Your experience of violence may have been for you what Elie Wiesel's first night in a Nazi death camp was for him: "moments which murdered my God and my soul" (quoted in Blumenthal 1991, 10).

John, a member of a Grown-Up Abused Children group, was adamant about his atheism. He insisted that the concept of God was phony. We assured him that belief in God was not required for participation in the group. During the next several months the topic was never a part of any of the discussions within the group. Nevertheless, during those months John opened himself to the caring of the members of the group. One day he confided to me that now he at least allowed for the possibility of a God. Several more months passed and John was convinced there was a God who had become an important part of his life.

This "conversion" was not the result of a rational apologetic but rather of loving, caring relationships. The constant anger and violence in John's family had not produced any experience of love to which he could connect the religious beliefs he heard discussed in the church that his abusive parents insisted he attend. The fear and distrust of others engendered by his family had deprived him of the possibility of experiencing love anywhere else. Only after experiencing care from members of the group was John able to learn the human trust necessary for religious belief and faith. Without such human experience as a basis for religious experience, faith was not accessible to him. To rephrase a well-known verse from the first letter of John: If you haven't been loved by people whom you have seen, how can you feel love from or for a God whom you have not seen? (See 1 John 4:20.)

Not all persons who have experienced abuse become confirmed atheists. You may believe in God, the Higher Power, but your concepts may lack much of what most people committed to the Jewish and Christian traditions consider important and meaningful—a loving, personal God. Your concept of God may be that of a stern taskmaster who is demanding and impossible to please, a harsh judge or king. God is primarily a transcendent force remote and removed from intimate relationship. For you God may be another force in your life, waiting for you to make a mistake for which you can be punished.

Even if your concept of God is not totally negative and demanding, it may lack personality and tenderness. Because you lack the experience to connect to what for many is a key attribute of God, that of a loving parent, your relationship to God may lack warmth or tenderness. Your belief may lack anything personal, sensitive, and enlivening. You may have no basis from which to call forth a joyful, loving response to a caring God. You may find it difficult to enter into a loving relationship with the God who is called Love.

Thus your spirituality, like much of your life, lacks the joy, warmth, and tenderness that grow out of trusting, caring relationships. Because you never experienced trust and caring, your life and its transcendent expression, spirituality, lack the warmth and gentleness that are the basis for true joy.

Proclamations about God as a loving father or praises of the blessings of a fatherly God may not attract, entice, or convince you to explore the riches of a life of faith. Such exhortations may not move you to open your life to the blessings, richness, and fulfillment some people claim are available through opening oneself to a loving God. You may also find it difficult to respond to any call for a relationship of love. You were assured by your parents that you were loved, but you found that their love entailed threats, pain, and abuse.

Like John, you may need first to experience human love, caring, and protection in order to relate to the religious concept of a loving parent. Nouwen himself acknowledges that, "We come to the growing awareness that we can love only because we have been loved first" (1975, 92). Your development of a prayer life also requires the development of a healthy personal and social life where you can experience the realities of human love and caring. Self-help support groups and twelve-step recovery groups provide excellent opportunities for such experiences. Participation in service and advocacy groups that deal with issues of family violence are excellent ways to experience and express love and caring that directly contradict your previous experience. They can enable you to create for yourself and others the caring community that makes real a loving God.

The development of personal friends and relationships may constitute important steps for your life of faith. Matthew Fox, the leading spokesperson for creation-centered spirituality, maintains that faith and trust are closely allied. He says, "Trust is not just a psychological issue—it is in fact a faith issue, indeed *the* faith issue." (1983, 83). He points out that the scriptural word tradition- ally translated as "faith" and commonly understood as "intellectual assent," in fact, means "trust." Experiencing the power of human trust and caring can provide a critical and indispensible foundation for your religious faith and spiritual development.

Not all survivors reject God as an alien concept. You may be among those who turned to God as Father from early childhood as a source of comfort and consolation. You may have been able to separate the abuse of your parents from the notion of a loving God who cared for and sustained you. You may be like some survivors who tell of seeking out churches during their childhood as places where they felt safe and where they could communicate with someone whom they knew loved them. Such times provided precious moments of security and peace. Their spiritual relationship with God the Father compensated for their lack of a caring family.

Even if you have made this latter response to God, questions may still haunt you: "Why didn't God do more? What is the good of a higher power, if it can't do more for me? If God loves me and wants the best for me—and this is what the best looks like—why should I care about this God? How can I respect a God who can't control evil?" We are back again to the issue of images of God and our expectations of God.

We all have expectations about how God should operate in the world or should make the world operate. We have our favorite modus operandi for God and become depressed, angry, or disbelieving when God fails to live up to our expectations. When we want a gentle, soothing God but instead get an exacting and demanding one, we feel betrayed. When the good things or feelings of life do not seem to be coming our way, we feel deceived and cheated. Our response ranges from blaming ourselves to blaming God.

We have already discussed the inappropriateness of blaming ourselves for things that are not our responsibility. If that is true, whom do we blame?

Can We Blame God?

The thought of blaming God may seem blasphemous. We have been taught that God is all-powerful, all-knowing, and all-loving. Everything that happens is for our well-being. "We know that all things work together for good for those who love God" (Rom. 8:28). The implication is that, if things are not going well, it is because we do not love enough or we do not understand God's ways.

Sure, we can all love more and try harder. It is true, we do not have perfect knowledge—God's ways are not ours, God's thoughts are not ours (Isa. 55:8), and we only see "in a mirror dimly" (1 Cor. 13:12). But to imply that it is our fault is to again blame the victim, and we have had enough of that.

So, what do we do? Are we caught in a religious catch-22? We are psychologically damaged if we blame ourselves. We are spiritually damned if we blame God. Neither option is appealing or healing. The scriptures indicate that there are many precedents for blaming God—at least challenging God to make the divine ways, which are supposed to be so all-fired great, clear to the mortals who are supposed to be sharing the divine image. Such attitudes toward God were known and acceptable to previous spokespersons for the faith community. It may be consoling and affirming to examine some of them.

Job is the best-known scripture character who was not hesitant to blame God. He was a real complainer—especially about God. His life was clearly a disaster and he was not afraid to express his dissatisfaction with the way things were going. He finally got God to come and deal with him face to face—man to God, as it were. God makes it clear that Job does not understand the profound, divine ways and that he is presumptuous to be so demanding, but God does not punish Job for his insolence. In fact, God restores what Job had lost.

The great Israelite leader, Moses, also was not reticent in complaining to God: "Why have you treated your servant so badly? Why have I not found favor in your sight? . . . If this is the way you are going to treat me, put me to death at once . . . and do not let me see my misery" (Num. 11:11–15). On another occasion Moses demanded, "O Lord, why does your wrath burn hot against your people?" And the Bible reports: "And the Lord changed his mind about the disaster that he planned to bring on his people" (Exod. 32:11, 14). Complaining about God is not only tolerated, it is rewarded. It gets results!

The Psalms are usually thought of as a collection of songs of praise, but many of them are filled with complaints about God and questions about the divine way in which things are done. The Psalms are

a most helpful resource for conversation with God about things that matter most . . . They articulate the entire gamut of Israel's speech to God, from profound praise to the utterance of unspeakable anger and doubt . . . [The psalms of lamentation] lead us into dangerous acknowledgment of how life really is. They lead us into the presence of God where everything is not polite and civil (Brueggemann 1984, 15, 53).

Jesus himself invoked one such psalm from the cross: "My God, my God, why have you forsaken me?" (Mark 15:35). These are the opening words of Psalm 22, which continues:

> Why are you so far from helping me,
>   from the words of my groaning?
> O my God, I cry by day, but you do not answer;
>   and by night, but find no rest. . . .
> But I am a worm, and not human;
>   scorned by others, and despised by the people.
> All who see me mock at me;
>   they make mouths at me, they shake their heads. . . .
> I am poured out like water,
>   and all of my bones are out of joint;
> my heart is like wax;
>   it is melted within my breast;
> my mouth is dried up like a potsherd,
>   and my tongue sticks to my jaws;
>   you lay me in the dust of death.
> For dogs are all around me;
>   a company of evildoers encircles me.
> My hands and feet have shriveled;
> I can count all my bones.
> They stare and gloat over me;
> they divide my clothes among themselves,
>   and for my clothing they cast lots.
>   (Psalm 22:1, 2, 6, 7, 14–18)

These sentiments are probably not unfamiliar to you as a survivor. There were many times when you felt forsaken and mocked and it seemed that no one, not even God, cared. Neither the psalmist, presumably King David, nor Jesus hesitated to complain to God and make their feelings part of their prayer life. They were part of a tradition that insisted that prayer was "communion [that] must be honest, open to criticism, and capable of transformation" (Brueggemann 1984, 173). They therefore considered it acceptable to demand, "Lord, do not be far away! . . . Come quickly to my aid" (Ps. 22:19). The psalmists could be very insistent. Psalm 13 begins with a litany of "How longs" (vs. 1–3):

> How long, O Lord? Will you forget me forever?
> How long will you hide your face from me?
> How long must I bear pain in my soul? . . .
> How long shall my enemy be exalted over me?

The litany concludes: "Consider and answer me, O Lord my God!"

The psalmists were not inclined to leave God to God's own devices. They were insolent enough to think they could tell God what to do: they made it clear what they thought God's ways should be. They were quick to state the rightness of their cause:

> Hear a just cause, O Lord;
>   attend to my cry;
> give ear to my prayer from lips free of deceit.
>   (Ps. 17:1)

They also admonished God to get involved:

> Why, O Lord, do you stand far off?
> Why do you hide yourself in times of trouble?
>   (Ps. 10:1)

> Contend, O Lord, with those who contend with me;
>   fight against those who fight against me!
> Take hold of shield and buckler,
>   and rise up to help me!
>   (Ps. 35:1–2)

Psalm 35 immediately proceeds to recommend solutions: "Let them be put to shame and dishonor. . . . Let them be like chaff before the wind. . . . Let their way be dark and slippery. . . . Let ruin come on them unawares" (vs. 4–6, 8).

Giving God such directives is also found in other psalms. Psalm 109 finds the author in difficult straits: "I am poor and needy, and my heart is pierced within me. . . . I am an object of scorn to my accusers" (vs. 22, 25). The author is quick to recommend actions for God: "Do not be silent, O God. . . . Save me according to your steadfast love. . . . Let my assailants be put to shame. . . . May my accusers be clothed with dishonor; may they be wrapped in their own shame as in a mantle" (vs. 1, 26, 28, 29).

In Psalm 94 the author even seeks to shame God into action: "O

Lord, . . . how long shall the wicked exult? . . . If the Lord had not been my help, my soul would soon have lived in the land of silence" (vs. 3, 17).

Such an approach to God is not common to traditional piety, but Rabbi Anson Laytner in his book, *Arguing With God,* points out that the Bible is filled with law-court patterns of argument with God voiced by leaders of the faith and preserved within the scriptures, which we call sacred. Building on this tradition David Blumenthal maintains: *"Given Jewish history and family violence as our generations have experienced them, protest is a proper religious affection and a theology of unrelenting challenge is a proper theology for us to have"* (1991, 14, emphasis his).

In conclusion we can say that it seems acceptable and even scripturally correct to be angry with God and to reproach God for some of the evils that have befallen you and to demand some redress. (Appendix C, "Psalms by a Survivor," contains contemporary lamentation psalms written by a survivor after she had read this part of the manuscript. She said she finally felt "permission" to express her anger toward God.) It may be psychologically necessary for you to blame God at some point in your healing journey, but that is not the end of the trek. Ultimately healthy living, whether spiritual or psychological, must go beyond anger and blame.

Try to Forgive God

Memory is a key element in human existence—it may be what makes us human. Remembering helps us put things in perspective, see them in relationship to other parts of our life, and perceive a totality to our existence. Earlier I suggested that keeping a journal might help you reconstruct memories of your past. A journal that records the positive experiences of your life as well as the negative can also be an important tool for reconstructing your relationship to God. It can help you recall all that God has done for you.

Memory is critical to our spiritual existence, our life of faith. It is central to the Jewish seder that remembers God's work in the exodus and celebrates God's faithfulness. Remembering is central to the Christian Eucharist, which is a prayer of thanksgiving for creation and redemption. Memory enables us to put our experiences of faith, our memories of God's work in our lives, into perspective—the good with the bad.

When Jesus cried out from the cross in the words of Psalm 22, he not only complained about his sense of abandonment, he likely was remembering also:

> Yet you are holy,
>> enthroned on the praises of
>> Israel.
> In you our ancestors trusted;
>> they trusted, and you delivered
>> them.
>
> (vs. 3–4)

This remembrance of God's caring and salvation in the past provided solace and consolation in his time of trial. It did not make the present pain any less, but it did enable Jesus to put it in perspective. By crying out in rage Jesus did not destroy his relationship with God, he retained it and focused it on the reality of the moment. Jesus did not like what was happening to him. It was not something he sought—he wanted it removed from him (Luke 22:42)—but he was also able to look beyond it, to see it within the total context of his relationship with God. By articulating his pain he was able to understand it within the broader picture of the plan he believed God had.

Jesus was explicit about his sense of abandonment, his disappointment and even his anger about the way God's divine plan was working out and the suffering it entailed for him. His words put their relationship in this time of suffering on an honest footing, just as such honesty is necessary for any relationship between friends or parents and children when hurt or disappointment occurs.

I want to reiterate our earlier discussion about whether God caused Jesus' suffering. Jesus' suffering and death were caused by the greed and hunger for power evidenced in the free will of the leaders. God simply allowed the free will of humans, given as a gift at creation, to be acted out. God did not interfere with the initial plan in creation. Much as we sometimes do not like it, "the doctrine of free will . . . is often referred to as one of the basic

principles of Judaism [and Christianity]. It is consistently assumed that God has taught man what is right and what is wrong
and left him to choose between the alternatives and the consequences. 'I have set before you life and death, the blessing and the
curse; choose life, then, that you and your descendants may live'
(Deuteronomy 30:19). . . . God does not predetermine whether a
man shall be righteous or wicked; that he leaves to man himself"
(Birnbaum, 41–42). It may be said that God was doing the best
that could be expected with a world and a people whose free will
had been tainted by sin.

Having said that, Jesus still felt abandoned in his suffering, just
as we all feel alone when we are in pain. Even when those close to
us are not responsible for our pain, we still feel disappointed and
sometimes angry at their inability to help us. We find we still have
to work to reestablish and reconcile our relationships.

Memory helps us confront the contradictions and paradoxes of
life—even the life of faith. Just as Susan alternately hugged and
hit the punching bag that represented her father, we humans
alternately hug and hate God. We are angry that God does not
control evil but grateful for *Emmanuel*, God with us. Christians
are grateful that God sent Jesus to, as the *Book of Common Prayer*
puts it, "share our human nature, to live and die as one of us, to
reconcile us to you, the God and Father of all," even though we
may prefer that God's role would take a different form.

Such an understanding evokes a God who is more accessible
but also more incomprehensible. God is all powerful and transcendent but also immanent, incarnate, and limited by the free
will of human beings. God is not only like a loving father, but also
a demanding though merciful judge. God is a shepherd who
guides and directs and also a mother hen who hovers and
protects. God creates and sustains but does not control. God
challenges and chides but also liberates, strengthens, and com-
forts. God becomes a full-fledged personality with all the lovable
yet infuriating characteristics we attribute to "personalities" in
our society. Our image of God includes all the contradictions,
paradoxes, and mystery we accept in our friends. We love them
and know they love us in spite of their failings and our failings.
Our memory enables us to accept and appreciate the complexity.
Our spiritual memory helps us realize that a single image of
God—and also all imaginable human combinations of images—

fails to express the magnitude of the divine. We then have a God without illusions, the God of the scriptures. As Walter Brueggemann puts it, "The God assumed by and addressed in [the] psalms is a God 'of sorrows, and acquainted with grief.' It is more appropriate to speak of this God in the categories of *fidelity* than of *immutability*, and when fidelity displaces immutability, our notion of God's sovereignty is deeply changed" (1984, 52, emphasis his).

When we accept the ambiguity of God we are forced to mourn the loss of an omnipotent God, who may have been more a product of our moments of helplessness than of our total religious experience. We also achieve a new level of psychological as well as spiritual maturity in our relationship with God. We are able to accept what we see as the good *and* the bad in God. This is an important developmental step that we humans have to achieve in our relationships with all significant others in our lives, including God. When we achieve it, we can celebrate a truly personal relationship with God, "Who anguishes yet cares, Who is concerned yet not controlling, Who feels pain and joy in interaction with us" (Blumenthal 1991, 15).

Whatever your feelings about God or however you respond to the idea of such a being—by total rejection, cautious but abstract acceptance or anxious seeking for security—it is important that you realize that a wide variety of images of God are affirmed within the Judeo-Christian tradition. It is important to develop a wide range of images of and relationships to God, remembering the good of life as well as the bad, the feelings of closeness as well as estrangement, the moments of security as well as of fear, the experience of God's anger as well as God's mercy. Then you can say with the psalmist:

> Wait for the Lord;
>> be strong, and let your heart take courage;
> wait for the Lord!
>
>> (Ps. 27:14)
>
> I waited patiently for the Lord;
>> he inclined to me and heard my cry.
> He drew me up from the desolate pit,
>> out of the miry bog,

> and set my feet upon a rock,
>   making my steps secure.
> He put a new song in my mouth,
>   a song of praise to our God.
>   (Ps. 40:1–2)

God may not always be doing things the way we want or as quickly as we might like, but we can always demand an explanation, request some clarification:

> Make me to know your ways, O Lord,
>   teach me your paths.
> Lead me in your truth, and teach me,
>   for you are the God of my salvation;
>   for you I wait all day long.
>   (Ps. 25:4–5)

The psalmists were not hesitant to declare:

> God is our refuge and strength,
>   a very present help in trouble.
> Therefore we will not fear,
>   though the earth should change,
>   though the mountains shake in the heart of the sea.
>   (Ps. 46:1–2)

They were not so naive as to believe that all was now well with the world. Even the most optimistic psalmists recognized that they still dwelt "among those who hate peace" (Ps. 120:6) and had to "walk through the darkest valley" (Ps. 23:4) but they believed God's goodness and mercy would accompany them (Ps. 23:6). That sustained them!

What we must remember is that such ambiguous experiences are common to all people and are not just a product of an abusive experience. Even the saints sometimes experienced God as distant or harsh. They called it the dark night of the soul. They complained about the cloud of unknowing within which they felt engulfed. They often experienced mistreatment at the hands of other people. Saint Therese of Lisieux is reported to have said that if this was the way God treated friends, there was little wonder God had so few.

Saints are those who are able to remember the broader picture of God's work in the world and in life. When they were able to remember the good experiences of life they were able to forgive God, to let loose the bad experiences so that those would not be the only things determining their attitudes. They reconciled themselves to the totality of God's work in their lives.

8 | Integration Through Prayer

Resolving your conflicts about God is only part of the effort required to unmask the illusions that hamper your spiritual growth. As a survivor, you may be empty of human pretensions and your mind may not be cluttered with frivolous human aspirations, but instead your heart may be riddled with undeserved guilt and your thoughts filled with frightening images. Your abusive experiences may have removed all semblance of pride and all sense of personal control, but those same experiences added layers of fear and instilled images of terror. The fears and anxieties generated in your family may intrude on your moments of contemplation, stifle the silence in your heart, and fill your solitude with distress and despair. You have difficulty focusing on anything but the fear and guilt you feel. The anxiety generated by your past floods the present and you cannot turn to God in trusting prayer.

One survivor told me that every time she attempted prayer she felt like she was being swallowed by a whirlpool. Each time she tried to pray, she had to pass through this fear before she could focus on her meditation. Other survivors describe the sensation of having holes in their bodies that they believe contain frightening images. As a survivor, before you can center yourself in prayer, you may need to confront your images and your emptiness and reestablish your wholeness and value. In the words of Paul, you must work to "not be conformed to this world [and all the negative messages you have received in it], but [to] be transformed by the renewing of your mind, so that you may discern what is the will of God—what is good and acceptable and perfect" (Rom. 12:2). What is "good and acceptable and perfect" is the you created by God.

Prayer: Spiritual Defiance

Therefore, your first spiritual goal as a survivor is not to cleanse yourself from pride and self-satisfaction (they already have been eradicated by your abuse) but to free yourself from anxiety and despair, to relieve your tensions and fears. This may need to be the first focus of your prayer. You may need to begin with what the spiritual writer Richard Foster calls "prayers of protection" (1988, 45), prayers that confront the evil that has been inflicted upon you and shield you from it. You may need to envision yourself surrounded by the saving light of God, wrapped in the white robe of righteousness or sealed with the cross of Christ. In this way you can protect yourself from the "roaring lion" of your past abuse that seeks to devour you (1 Peter 5:8). Wrapped in the robe of righteousness you can withstand the buffeting of whirlpools and the frightening flashbacks of your abuse. Armed with the light of God you will find the strength to investigate the dark holes within you. (See Appendix B, "Guided Meditations for Survivors," for examples of meditations for this purpose.) You may discover there critical forgotten parts of your life—the much-discussed "inner child"—that can profit from the healing light of God. That light can illumine the repressed recesses of your personality and spirituality and help you develop them to their fullness.

Do not be concerned that such visual prayers are not what your prayer life should be about. They are important acts of connecting with God and may constitute the most important "work" of prayer you will do. Thomas Merton has written, "Meditation has no point and no reality unless it is firmly rooted in life" (1969, 39). "[G]enuine communion with God is never removed from the seasons, times, and crises of life" (Brueggemann 1984, 170). A central fact of your life was your abuse. Your prayer appropriately should not deny but be rooted in that reality, for prayer is "the theater in which the diseased spirituality that we have contracted from the powers can most directly be discerned, diagnosed, and treated. . . . [It is] spiritual defiance of what is, in the name of what God has promised" (Wink 1990, 10). Having achieved solidarity with your pain, prayer now becomes your way to treat that pain in order to envision and enact a new reality for yourself and your world. The world needs more prayer rooted in the reality of family violence if its terrible presence is to be discerned and defied and the peace that God has promised is to become the new reality!

Another approach to the frightening images of your past might be to seek to clear them from your mind so that your heart can be truly open for God to be revealed. In order to accomplish this, a special kind of cleansing may be necessary. To achieve the concentration necessary to do this it will be helpful to acquaint yourself with the physical mechanics of prayer and meditation. You may need to learn practical techniques of breathing, focused imaging, and relaxation that can help you eliminate unwanted thoughts. This process is often difficult so you may need to find someone who can lead you through the steps of relaxation procedures. Secular counselors as well as spiritual directors are often proficient teachers of these processes. These techniques, more common to Eastern meditation, are effective methods for emptying one's mind of haunting, negative images and messages. Then you can begin to fill your mind with new messages and images. You can begin to focus on the positive in your life.

Direct efforts to eradicate negative images is only one way to deal with them. You can also fight such images by replacing them. You can use similar techniques to create new images of peace and safety—a favorite pastoral scene, Jesus embracing you as a child or talking with you as an adult—or to focus your attention on a single word or short phrase—a word or phrase of personal affirmation, a statement of union with the loving God or a favorite passage of scripture. An effective prayer form for this purpose is the simple "Breath Prayer," which addresses God by whatever name is meaningful and comfortable to you (Father, Lord, Jesus, Higher Power) and then articulates in a short statement (six to eight syllables) what you most want or need at that time. Your petition could be, "Let me feel your peace," "Guide me in your will," "Let me know your love," or whatever you feel you need (DelBane 1981, 27–47). Repeating this prayer over and over again, just as one breathes, can displace images of loneliness and distress.

Counselors and spiritual directors can be particularly helpful in this process. They can teach you and lead you through visualization techniques by which you replace the fearful images and messages within you, release the tensions that bind you, and fill the gaps you experience with images of God's loving care. They can also be your contact with God when all else seems to fail. Their loving care for you can image God when you cannot do so for yourself.

Because of your abuse experience you have been disengaged from many of the illusions that commonly hinder spiritual development. Any images of human immortality and power you may have had were destroyed by the violence and threats you experienced. Any notions of pride and arrogance have been dispelled. You are empty and ready for the enlivening power of God. In the words of Matthew Fox, you have been emptied so you are "vulnerable to beauty and truth, to justice and compassion, . . . truly hollow and hallowed channel[s] for divine grace" (1983, 172) Your spiritual challenge is to fill the gaps in your life with the loving power of God.

Prayer: The Creation of Courage

However, spiritual growth demands more than learning techniques. Prayer is more than techniques for feeling good about yourself or even about God, for filling the gaps in yourself or your world. Prayer is not merely about escaping the fears and agonies in your life, it is also about confronting and transforming those fears, living through them with the courage by which you reclaim yourself from fear and become fully human. Paul Tillich, one of the leading theologians of the twentieth century, maintained that the issue of courage is "rooted in the whole breadth of human existence. . . . The courage to be is the ethical act in which man affirms his own being in spite of those elements of his existence which conflict with his essential self-affirmation" (1952, 1, 3). This is a major focus of the Bible, something recognized as an important and ongoing concern for all people of God. Judith Lechman points out that there are nearly five hundred calls to "be not afraid" in the Hebrew and Christian scriptures (1988, xii). For you, as a survivor of family violence, that call has special urgency. You have many conflicts about your self-worth to confront. You have many debilitating experiences of fear to overcome.

Turning to God in prayer can help you confront the darkness and pain of your life and fill it with the "light of life" (John 8:12). It can strengthen you to embrace the desert of the exodus and the despair of the cross and transform them into a land flowing with milk and honey and a new life. Even as you affirm the blessed creation of which you are a part, you must acknowledge that the "whole creation has been groaning in labor pains" (Rom. 8:22). Such acknowledgment does not mean you accept it as an unchangeable, perpetual reality. You continue to hope for the redemption of your body. "For in hope we were saved" (Rom. 8:24). Your hope can create your new reality because

> History belongs to the intercessors, who believe the future into being. . . . The future belongs to whoever can envision in the manifold of its possibilities a new and desirable possibility, which faith then fixes upon as inevitable. That is the politics [and psychology] of hope. Hope envisions its future and then acts as if that future is then irresistible, thus helping to create the reality for which it longs. (Wink 1990, 11)

Prayer can create this new future in sometimes surprising ways. One survivor who regularly used the Breath Prayer tells of the time she began to pray, "Lord, hold me in your arms." As she closed her eyes and recited this prayer she had the image of God crushing her. She became very angry and began to fight back, beating God with her fists. She wanted to kill God. The more she fought the more God held her tightly in what became a loving embrace. She experienced God's loving embrace in a new way. Her prayer was answered with mind-boggling immediacy. The reality for which she longed was created.

Your prayer is also an expression of your commitment and struggle to be fully human in the face of the impossible circumstances created by abuse in your family. "Real prayer is life creating and life changing. . . . To pray is to change. Prayer is the central avenue God uses to transform us" (Foster 1988, 33). It is your effort to understand and strive for what God intended. Even as you feel overwhelmed by darkness, you must remember that "darkness is not dark to [God]; the night is as bright as the day; for darkness is as light to [God]" (Ps. 139:12). Even as you feel weak you need to remember that "the Spirit helps us in our weakness; for we do not know how to pray as we ought, but that very Spirit intercedes with sighs too deep for words" (Rom. 8:26). Your healing and your spiritual growth will come from confronting the confining darkness of your anxiety and envisioning the liberating light of life.

Henri Nouwen points out that the Latin word for anxiety is *angustia*, which means narrowness (1975, 89). By defying the anxiety (narrowness) imposed by your abuse experience, you will be able to confront the questions life has presented (an important part of the first movement of the spiritual life), let go of your anger (the forgiveness involved in the second movement), and be freed from illusions to receive new life from the God of all life (the third movement). You will achieve the wholeness (holiness) and largeness of heart (courage) which will enable you to embrace the whole of life—the life to which you have been called but of which you have been deprived by family violence. Then you can say that "neither death, nor life, nor angels, nor rulers, nor things present, nor things to come, nor powers, nor height, nor depth, nor anything else in all creation [even the violence of your family], will be able to separate [you] from the love of God" (Rom. 8:38–39).

You must, however, beware of expecting prayer to be an instantly clear guide to new options and opportunities in your life—new vistas of growth and development. P. T. Forsyth points out that "Prayer is to religion what original research is to science" (Foster 1988, 38). Prayer is the process of opening oneself to God and trying to hear and understand all that God may be calling us to do. It means approaching God without preconceived notions and without set timetables for answers to our needs and problems. The anxieties (narrowness) created by abusive experience and the frightening lack of control it engendered may prompt you to see every thought you have in prayer, every opportunity which presents itself after you have opened your life to God, as a sure sign from God of the divine will. Richard Foster points out that "the fact that God speaks to us does not guarantee that we rightly understand the message" (1988, 140). The challenge for all people of faith is to apply God's gifts of intellect, talent, and personal preference and inclination as critical parts of the process of discernment. These gifts are called forth and enhanced, not eliminated, by prayer.

As a survivor you must beware of returning to the powerless mind-set that you learned in your abusive home and that made you feel that you were incompetent and that your personal likes and dislikes were not important. Because of the powerlessness you learned in your home, it may be easy for you to fall into "an uncritical form of objectivism about God that assigns everything to God, that empties [your] own life of dignity, worth, and authority, and that imagines that everything is settled on the unchanging terms of divine sovereignty" (Brueggemann 1989, 46). As we have seen above, such an unchanging, uninvolved deity is not the God of scripture who hears the cries of suffering people. The God of scripture respects the gifts and insights of the people God created and responds to their needs.

You may need to be especially cautious about religious groups that appear to provide quick and easy answers to all of life's problems and sure insight into the will of God. Such an authoritarian model may seem comfortable to you because it continues a life pattern of outside control over your life that is familiar to you. Such a system frees you from having to pay attention to the very thoughts and feelings your families told you were evil and prideful. You must remind yourself that God gave you a brain and personal preferences as part of the gift of creation. They are part of who God called you to be and are a legitimate part of your prayer. They must be taken seriously, not ignored. Even the medieval theologian, Thomas Aquinas, maintained that God's grace does not negate human gifts and experiences but fulfills and perfects them. They are a way God speaks to you—listen to them! They express what you are called to have the courage to be!

As a survivor, the illusions you must unmask are not of pride but of a false sense of worthlessness, not of power but impotence, not audacity but fear. Your prayer must focus on affirming your worth, empowering your life, and finding the courage to express your dignity and live out your value.

Courage for New Life

Living out your value is the spiritual challenge for you as a survivor. In your spiritual development you have confronted the contradictions imposed on you by your abusive family, you have challenged the religious images that may have contributed to your abuse and continued the abusive pattern outside your home. You have examined and reassessed the tenets of your faith. As you undertook the disturbing task of scrutinizing your beliefs and questioning and arguing with your God, you uncovered a new and deeper form of relationship with God. As you plumbed the depths of your anger—even at God—you may have been surprised by the grace of a new understanding of God and a new understanding with God. You developed a more mature relationship, one that allows for differences, variation, and growth. As you dared to speak the psalms of lament and express your own prayers of anger, you may have discovered deep reservoirs of affection. Your anger turned to understanding, your hostility to trust, and your "mourning into dancing" (Ps. 30:11). You cried out in pain and found healing. Your doubts, for all their intensity, did not end in atheism. Instead, they led to more passionate address and new faith. You discovered that your abuse turned your "eyes from looking at vanities," gave you new life in God's ways, and confirmed you in God's promise (Ps. 119:37–38).

Not everything in your life is now perfect. You have good times and bad. Your spiritual life does not always follow a straight line or a smooth path. But you realize that such ambivalence and vacillation are part of the spiritual reality for all people, part of the process of spiritual growth, just as it is a part of psychological growth. Psalm 40 marvelously exemplifies this. It begins by describing the condition of all survivors, waiting "patiently for the Lord" (v. 1). God finally comes and draws "me up from the desolate pit . . . [and] put[s] a new song in my mouth" (vs. 2, 3). The psalmist is as happy as "those who make the Lord their trust" (v. 4), and he tells "the glad news of deliverance in the great congregation . . . [speaks] of your [God's] faithfulness and your salvation" (vs. 9, 10). But such happiness is not constant, soon "evils have encompassed me without number" (v. 12). God again has to be called on to "make haste to help" (v. 13); those who "seek to snatch away my life . . . [have to] be turned back and brought to dishonor" (v. 14). The psalmist continues to feel "poor and needy" but acknowledges that "the Lord takes thought for me . . . [and is] my help and my deliverer" (v. 17). Psalm 40 has been identified by many commentators as a thanksgiving for deliverance and a prayer for help. That is also an apt description of the continuing cycle of the spiritual life.

The process of spiritual growth, the task of healing from abuse, is not an easy one. "Many are the afflictions of the righteous, but the Lord rescues them from them all" (Ps. 34:19). The consoling factor is that there is healing, there is growth, there is increased "strength of soul" (Ps. 138:3). You can become, as Linda Sanford says in her marvelous book by that title, strong at the broken places. I cannot tell you when it will happen, it varies for everyone, but there is a turning point, a moment of grace when your pleas turn into praise, your anxieties dissolve into thanksgivings and the disarray of your life finds new direction. A time does come when, even though "the arrogant utterly deride" you, you are still able to remember God's promise, which provides you hope and comfort in distress and gives you life (see Ps. 119: 49–51). You then "have an answer for those who taunt" you for you trust in God's word and "walk at liberty" (see Ps. 119: 42–45). God then ceases to be distant or abstract but rather present and personal. You are able to

> taste and see that the Lord is good;
> happy are those who take refuge in him.
> (Ps. 34:8)

APPENDIX A
Religious Messages That Destroy Spirituality

Many teachings within the Jewish and Christian traditions have not been helpful to persons who were being abused in their families. Very often certain passages of scripture have been used to justify or rationalize the power, control, and even violence exhibited by dedicated members of churches and synagogues. While these teachings have not created the problem of family abuse, simplistic and distorted interpretations of some passages have contributed to a cultural mind-set that overlooks and even justifies family violence. They have also made it difficult for victims to break the cycle of violence and for survivors to heal the spiritual wounds created by the abuse. These passages need to be interpreted in their broader context so that they can become sources of spiritual growth—not decay.

Spare the Rod and Spoil the Child

Although the oft quoted axiom "spare the rod and spoil the child" is not a direct quotation from scripture, there is much biblical basis for such a statement. Proverbs and its deuterocanonical counterpart, Ecclesiasticus, are great sources of pithy sayings to guide one's daily life, one's family life, and especially parents' relationship to their children. The advice given seems to favor a strict orientation and to approve of physical discipline. Jesus Ben Sirach, the author of Ecclesiasticus, admonishes his parental readers, "Do you have children? Discipline them, and make them obedient from their youth" (7:23). He also encourages them to be steadfast in their efforts to keep their children in line: "Of the following things do not be ashamed, and do not sin to save face: . . . frequent disciplining of children" (42:1, 5).

The scriptural assumption seems to be that children are naturally troublesome and unruly and that they are best brought into line by the rod: "Folly is bound up in the heart of a boy, but the rod of discipline drives it far away" (Prov. 22:15). "The rod and reproof give wisdom, but a mother is disgraced by a neglected child" (Prov. 29:15). Some authors have suggested that the rod referred to is the shepherd's rod and staff, which in Psalm 23 is a source of guidance and comfort (Bingham 1986, 59). However, the references to this "rod of discipline" seem to be quite frequent and often harsh: "Do not withhold discipline from your children; if you beat them with the rod, they will not die. If you beat them with the rod, you will save their lives from Sheol" (Prov. 23:13–14). Although guidance may be necessary and the intentions may be good, the use of this rod as it is described does not sound particularly comforting. The authors of Proverbs and Ecclesiasticus are clear that the purpose of the beatings are for love: "Those who spare the rod hate their children, but those who love them are diligent to discipline them" (Prov. 13:24); "He who loves his son will whip him often" (Ecclus. 30:1). Such beatings are nonetheless painful, and unless administered judiciously and with great care, can inflict physical and psychological harm.

The biblical assumption that children are naturally troublesome has had a long-standing effect on child-rearing practices. Philip Greven in his study of seventeenth and eighteenth century child-rearing practices discovers many of the same principles and documents incredibly harsh and abusive disciplinary tactics proudly reported by evangelical pastors. Some of the child-rearing principles that prevailed in that time included this observation by John Robinson: "Surely there is in all children, though not alike, a stubbornness, and stoutness of mind arising from natural pride, which must, in the first place, be broken and beaten down; that so, the foundation of their education being laid in humility and tractableness, other virtues may, in the time, be built thereon." To succeed in this, "children's wills and wilfulness [must] be restrained and repressed" (Greven 1977, 37). As John

Wesley put it, "Break their wills that you may save their souls" (Greven 1977, 35). This will-breaking, Greven reports, was often accomplished by severe beatings or by long periods of deprivation of food or physical contact. Cotton Mather on the other hand "knew that the most effective method for ensuring the compliance of children with the wills of their parents was not beatings but guilt and shame" (Greven 1977, 52).

Despite the fact that modern psychology has provided insights into the process of child development that challenge the rationale for such disciplinary practices, many of them are still used with the same justification. Despite the fact that psychologists have learned that violent discipline only controls unacceptable behavior for as long the threat of violence is present, corporal punishment is still a widely accepted child-rearing practice among all socioeconomic groups. All too often children are still told that the beatings they receive are "for your own good," that they are being given "so you will learn," or that they are a sign of how much your parents "love" you.

Such an interpretation of the scriptures—one that has not been sufficiently challenged by most religious leaders—can make it difficult for an abused child to look to a church or synagogue for relief from abusive parents. An awareness of these scriptural maxims, sermons heard extolling parenthood and admonishing "honor," as well as parents' invocations of the scriptural proverbs, make it difficult for victims to acknowledge and discuss the negative and even hostile feelings they may have about their parents.

Honor Your Father and Your Mother

Probably the most familiar of the Ten Commandments is that which orders children to honor their fathers and mothers. It is the one commandment that most people can quote without hesitation. It is also the only one of the Ten Commandments to which a promise is attached: "Honor your father and your mother, so that your days may be long in the land that the Lord your God is giving you" (Exod. 20:12).

Societal awareness as well as scriptural expression give special emphasis to this commandment, emphasis based on the assumption that every child has a unique relationship to his or her parents. This is commonly conceived as a natural obligation, an obligation rooted in the fact of birth. As the author Jesus Ben Sirach put it, "With all your heart honor your father, and do not forget the birth pangs of your mother. Remember that it was of your parents you were born; how can you repay what they have given to you?" (Ecclus. 7:28–30). The realization that one's physical existence stems from one's parents and that the early maintenance of one's life depends on the nurture and care of parents gives natural weight to the religious admonition to honor one's father and mother. Any thought of action that fails to respect the source of one's life and recognize one's total dependence on one's parents appears to exhibit particularly invidious ingratitude. It seems to go against everything that is good, true and natural. "It is a disgrace for children not to respect their mother" (Ecclus. 3:11).

The Bible is quick to support that view. The covenant codes in Exodus state clearly, "Whoever strikes father or mother shall be put to death" (21:15). Two verses later the message gets even stronger, "Whoever curses father or mother shall be put to death" (21:17). Leviticus connects the penalty with an even lesser affront to one's parents: "All who curse father or mother shall be put to death; having cursed father or mother, their blood is upon them" (20:9). God seems to mean business about respect for one's parents.

As an abused child you may have found this commandment frequently reinforced by civil and religious social structures. Many institutions of society are designed to strengthen family life and in the process they exalt the role of parents. One of the more difficult philosophical issues confronted by child abuse prevention advocates is that of the presumed independence and sanctity of the family. One of the more serious debates revolves around the inherent rights of parents over their children, including the right of and the need for parents to discipline their children. If child protection workers intervened in your family, they may have been accused of interfering with your parents' "God given rights" to raise and discipline you as they saw fit. Much of the basis for these "rights" is found in Proverbs and Ecclesiasticus.

Despite such common interpretations, the pithy sayings attributed to Solomon and Sirach—no matter how harsh many seem to be—must be understood within the context of the purpose of the wisdom literature. The wisdom of the Lord that the books attempt to communicate to foolish humans is based on "the fear of the Lord [which] is glory and exultation, and gladness and a crown of rejoicing. The fear of the Lord delights the heart and gives gladness and joy and long life" (Ecclus. 1:11–12). These books of wisdom were written "For learning about wisdom and instruction, for understanding words of insight, for gaining instruction in wise dealing, righteousness, justice, and equity" (Prov. 1:2–3). Abuse and violence are hardly the ways of "wise dealing, righteousness, justice, and equity." Physical harm and psychological devastation associated with violent discipline cannot be reconciled with such purposes.

Parents do need to instruct their children, to discipline (train) them and share with them the insights they will need in later life, but such a process should not produce anguish, anger, and fear. Rather it should produce "a fair garland for your head, and pendants for your neck" (Prov. 1:9). The various tidbits of child-rearing advice contained in these books should be understood in this context. To take specific verses out of that loving framework is to distort the intent of the sages who were attempting to provide practical applications for the loving wisdom of God in daily life.

The author of the Christian letter to the Hebrews also acknowledges the need for such discipline because even God "disciplines us for our good" (12:10). The author goes on to say that "discipline always seems painful rather than pleasant at the time, but later it yields the *peaceful fruit of righteousness* to those who have been *trained* by it" (12:11, emphasis mine). Once again, the purpose of discipline (not necessarily corporal punishment) is training, a training that instills peacefulness, not fear and trembling. Any other effect is a distortion of discipline!

However, it cannot be denied that many religiously motivated people have taken these scriptural passages out of context and used them to justify abusive and domineering behavior. The authors of the wisdom literature and Hebrews may not have adequately recognized the creative ability of humans to twist otherwise sound advice to justify personal preferences and propensities. They may not have provided adequate controls and correctives for the tendencies of humans and even parents to use their positions of authority in harmful ways. As an abused child, you learned that even parental power can corrupt absolutely.

One of the important messages promulgated by Jesus during his ministry was that all power was to be used in service to others, that the use of any power was to be guided by gentleness, caring and concern. The apostle Paul recognized that Jesus had offered a new model for relationships between superiors and subordinates. Although unequal relationships do exist and may even serve useful purposes for the good ordering of society, such distinctions between individuals are not justification for distancing or disdain between people or for the oppression of one person or group by another.

"Let each of you remain in the condition in which you were called" (1 Cor. 7:20). For Paul that admonition was true even if one were a slave, for that condition was not the determining factor in one's relationship to God or even in one's relationship to one's master. One's social condition could remain the same because what was important was that the nature of the relationship had been changed. The slave should love and serve the master just as the master should love and serve the slave. As oppressive and restrictive as this may seem to us today, Paul believed that the social relationship was not what was important, but the way the relationship was lived out in practice (see Eph. 6:5–9).

However, this new kind of relationship or association not dependent on social standing but on mutual respect, love, and concern has not always been lived out in practice. If this new reality was going to work, new guidelines were needed; a new sense of mutuality was necessary. Paul recognized that correctives were required in the standard ways that relationships were exercised. He recognized that there were excesses and harmful aspects to the way superiors related to their subordinates, even the way parents related to their children.

Paul did not deny that children needed to obey their parents. He supported his teaching, "Children, obey your parents in the Lord, for this is right" (Eph. 6:1), with the commandment to honor one's parents (Eph. 6:2–3). However, he recognized that it was possible for parents to be excessive in their attempts to discipline their children, and he was quick to point out that mutuality is required in this relationship: "Fathers, do not provoke your children to anger, but bring them up in the discipline and instruction of the Lord," or as the Jerusalem Bible translates that passage, "correct them and guide them as the Lord does" (Eph. 6:4, see also Col. 3:20–21). This is, of course, the same Lord who gave himself unto death for those he loved. Paul is offering a new model for parent-child relationships, a model of gentle, caring love, not abusive, threatening "love." Such a model does not allow for ridicule and denigration, much less beatings and abuse.

It might be well to point out here that we humans have had trouble living up to Paul's ideal for social relationships. We have learned that we could not leave a slave "in the condition in which [he was] called." If slaves and masters were going to have the kind of relationship Paul recommended, their social inequality had to be changed. We humans could not properly manage our power over another.

Society as a whole is now learning something that you who were abused have known for a long time—in many families the power of parents needs to be controlled externally. It is not safe to leave children "in the condition in which [they have been] called."

Rabbinic teachers were also great believers in parental authority but they did not consider it an absolute, they recognized other factors. "R. Eleazar b. Mattai said: If my father were to say to me, 'Give me some water to drink,' and I had at that moment a command [of the Law] to fulfil, then I should omit the honor due a father, and fulfil the command . . ." (Montifiore 1963, 501). David Blumenthal points out that "obedience is limited because the parent cannot ask a child to violate the Torah . . . [T]here is a trans-parental authority to which one can, indeed must, appeal if the parent is wrong" (1990).

Jesus also affirmed such a trans-parental authority: "Whoever loves father or mother more than me is not worthy of me" (Matt. 10:37, see also, Luke 14:26). He even recommended that when it came to a choice between following him and burying a dead parent, "the dead [should] bury their own dead" (Luke 9:60).

Blumenthal also maintains that the *Talmud Torah* "implies a whole series of attitudes and behaviors towards children, for they are the bearers of Torah through time until the coming of the messiah. The sacred role of children . . . protects them in rabbinic teaching, despite the patriarchal and otherwise authoritarian social structure of the tradition. . . . To abuse a child is to inhibit the spread of Torah, to destroy the image of the divine, and to place an impediment in the way of the messiah" (1990).

Such reflections challenge many long-held beliefs about the integrity of the family, the autonomy of parental power, and the appropriateness of physical discipline within the family. They call for an examination of such beliefs and the feelings attendant upon them. This is a difficult and time-consuming process for society, but it is important one. If society is going to be responsive to the survivors in its midst, it must engage in this process. It must seriously examine its assumptions and convictions. Once society has engaged in such a process, it can begin to explore alternative forms of parental discipline, alternatives to isolated families, alternatives to denying the reality of abuse in our society.

The recognition of the need for such alternatives will open the door for discussion and sharing about problems within families. Then children presently being victimized as well as those who have survived such treatment will know that there is a difference between honoring and respecting your parents. Blumenthal points out "the rabbis distinguish between 'respecting' which is the 'don'ts' and 'honoring' which is the 'do's.' Thus, one must go out of one's way to be loving and kind with one's parents. However, not everyone is privileged to be able to so 'honor' his or her parents: they may not deserve it, they may not accept it, etc. But, everyone must respect her or his parents: don't contradict them in public, don't sit in their place, etc. . . ." (1990). This distinction must be accepted and affirmed within the religious community which admonishes "Honor Your Father and Your Mother."

Wives, Be Subject

Battered women are also part of the web of family violence affected by some teachings within the Jewish and Christian traditions. The common interpretation and application of both the Hebrew and Christian scriptures affirms the superiority of husbands over their wives. One of the common scriptural words for marriage (*ba'al*) focuses on the notion of ownership and lordship. The book of Genesis wastes little time telling women that their husbands "shall rule over [them]" (3:16). A favorite Christian passage is Paul's admonition: "Wives, be subject to your husbands" (Eph. 5:22). Frequently such passages are invoked to justify the rights of husbands to dominate and control their wives—sometimes even by violent means.

These passages, combined with those that affirm the sanctity and indissolubility of marriage—"Therefore what God has joined together, let no one separate" (Matt. 19:6)—imposed a heavy burden of guilt on anyone trying to break out of a violent family setting. To do so violated two important religious tenets. It meant stepping out of one's proper role with one's husband and breaking up a marriage.

Let us first consider the role of a woman in the family. This issue is not merely a problem of outdated theology that has long ago been abandoned or of theology that is relegated to extremely conservative, fundamentalist groups. The theology we are about to discuss is alive and well in much of mainline Christianity as well.

A friend who works at a battered women's shelter recently shared with me a "holy card" that a woman at the shelter had received from her pastor when she went to him for help. The card was beautifully printed and laminated. It contained "A Wife's Daily Prayer" on one side and "Ten Rules for a Happy and Successful Wife" on the other. The prayer petitioned God for cheerfulness, unselfishness, patience, and several other laudatory virtues. The rules were:

1. Avoid arguments. Your husband has his share from other sources.
2. Don't nag.
3. Don't drink or eat to excess.
4. If you offend your husband, always ask forgiveness before you retire.
5. Compliment your husband liberally. It makes him a better husband.
6. Budget wisely together. Live within your income.
7. Be sociable and go out with your husband.

8. Dress neatly and attractively for your husband and keep your home clean and cheerful.
9. Keep your household troubles to yourself.
10. Pray together and stay together.

The virtues are worthy enough—few of us are opposed to cheerfulness. Even some of the rules are not half bad. The problem is that the admonitions are directed only toward the wife and not to the husband and wife together. The tone of these rules and the way they are directed only at the wife exhibit a patriarchal theology that ought to offend both men and women. As a male, I object to the implications about the delicate male ego contained in the rule: "Compliment your husband liberally." These rules assume a subservient role for the wife and lack any sensitivity to the mutuality and complementarity that ought to be a part of a healthy relationship.

What is atrocious about this "holy card" is that it was given to a woman who was being battered by her husband. In effect, she was being told, "Go back to your husband and be cheerful in the face of his beatings; patiently suffer his abuse." This simple act by a pastor proclaimed loudly and clearly an antiwoman theology that condones violence in the family. It is little wonder that many shelter workers accuse Jewish and Christian teachings of contributing to family violence. It is little wonder that if you were abused by your husband and have received similar counsel, you have little or no time for this kind of religion.

When one examines the scriptures that are the basis of Jewish and Christian theology, it cannot (and need not) be denied that there is a passage in Genesis that says that husbands shall rule their wives. However, that line needs to be understood in context. The immediate context is that the statement is part of the curse laid upon Adam and Eve for their failure to live up to the requirements of the creation covenant. The statement is not made as part of a blessed promise but as a condemnation brought about by sin. The control of man over woman is the result of a distortion of relationships, not the ideal to be sought in relationships between men and women. Such a role relationship is not a blessing for either party.

To understand the ideal, one need only consider the broader context of the creation story. The two accounts of the creation of man and woman make it abundantly clear that both are special creations: "In the image of God he created them; male and female he created them" (Gen. 1:27); and that they both share much in common, "bone of my bones and flesh of my flesh" (Gen. 2:23). When such unique creatures are bound so intimately together, neither is intended to be subordinate to the other, neither ought to be controlled by the other, especially by mutually degrading violence.

Sin may have seriously damaged the ideal relationship that God intended between men and women, but that is not a justification for continuing and furthering the disruption of relationships. The effects of sin are realities in our world, but they do not constitute the ideals by which we ought to guide our lives and form our relationships. The ideal to be affirmed and sought is that of unity and mutuality.

On the other hand, Paul's admonition, "Wives, be subject to your husbands, as you are to the Lord" (Eph. 5:22), cannot be discounted as part of a curse. He is clearly stating an ideal to be sought. However, what is so often quoted is only part of that ideal. The whole passage speaks about a mutual relationship between husbands and wives, not just a relationship of wives to husbands. The whole section begins, "Be subject to one another out of reverence for Christ" (Eph. 5:21), and goes on to speak of a mutual relationship between husbands and wives.

It should be noted that the word that is most commonly translated "subject" would more appropriately be translated "defer" or "accommodate" (Bingham 1968, 57). The ideal Paul is trying to communicate is mutual sensitivity and responsiveness, the kind of "more than halfway" willingness to give on the part of both parties that is essential for any successful marriage. Paul goes on to hold up Jesus as the model of giving and service toward which both husbands and wives ought to strive.

The Reverend Marie Fortune points out that most of Paul's passage on marriage (Eph. 5:21–29) is directed to husbands. "Nine of the verses are directed toward husbands' responsibilities in marriage; only three of the verses refer to wives' responsibilities and one refers to both. Yet, contemporary interpretation often focuses only on the wives and often misuses those passages to justify the abuse of wives by their husbands" (1983, 57). If you have been battered in your marriage, you know how true Fortune's final statement is. You probably heard this scripture quoted through flailing fists.

It cannot be denied that abuse occurs in many marriages. What cannot be claimed is that Paul in any way condones it. Instead his recommendation is "husbands should love their wives as they do their own bodies. . . . For no one ever hates his own body, but he nourishes and tenderly cares for it" (Eph. 5:28–29). In another of his letters Paul indicates that he recognizes the propensity for men of his time to be abusive to their wives. He admonishes, "Husbands, love your wives and never treat them harshly" (Col. 3:19).

Paul's ideal of mutual accommodation also extends to the area of sexual relations within marriage. Mutual deference to one another in all matters means that no member of the marriage relationship has "rights" over the other that are not freely given. Equality and mutuality within marriage means that all aspects of the relationship, even those related to conjugal relations and sexual access, must be determined by mutual consent. Wives and husbands each have the right to refuse sexual relations. There is a mutual hearing of both rights and duties. As Paul put it in his first letter to the Corinthians: "The husband should give to his wife her conjugal rights, and likewise the wife to her husband. For the wife does not have authority over her own body, but the husband does; likewise the husband does not have authority over his own body, but the wife does" (7:3–4). Thus, any rights within marriage are mutual and parallel. They do not exist without the consent of the partner. Persons in a marriage have entered into a unique relationship where all their personal rights are equally shared with and controlled by their marriage partner. They truly are not two but one flesh. The man is admonished to "cling" to his wife (Gen. 2:24), not dominate her or be dominated by her. Marriage is to be a relationship of equals.

When a partner insists on claiming his personal "right" without regard for his partner's wishes, he is breaking the unity and mutuality essential to the sacredness of the marriage bond. The bond is broken because he insists on his rights as a separate and distinct person, not as part of a partnership. He ceases to operate as part of a larger whole. He ceases to function as a married person.

To summarize, the role of a woman in a marriage is not that of an inferior subject required to put up with whatever kind of treatment a husband chooses to exercise. Women are equal partners with mutually shared rights as well as responsibilities. They are "companions" rather than merely "helpers." Phyllis Trible points out that "companion" is a more accurate translation of the Hebrew word in Genesis 2:20 usually translated "helper." It does not connote the more subordinate and inferior meanings associated with helper. As she says, "In the Hebrew scripture, this word ('ezer) often describes God as the superior who creates and saves Israel. . . . According to Yahweh God, what the earth creature needs is a companion, one who is neither subordinate nor superior; one who alleviates isolation through identity" (Trible 1978, 90). If a woman is going to relieve the isolation of her husband, she must be regarded as an equal with important ideas and resources to contribute, not merely as a subservient housewife whose only purpose is to respond to the demands of her husband. A woman cannot be an equal companion if she is subject to fear and intimidation in her relationship. When the relationship is ruled by threats and violence, the purpose of the relationship has ceased to exist.

Yes, women have an important role in marriage and need to be accommodating to their husbands. But that accommodation needs to go both ways. Wives are not to be submissive and subservient, and certainly they are not to be the recipients of violence. There is nothing in the Jewish and Christian traditions that approves of violence directed towards persons and especially persons committed to the special, loving, and mutual marriage relationship.

The Jewish and Christian communities have a long way to go to overcome the incomplete and distorted interpretations and applications to which many of the passages of their scriptures have been subjected. Unfortunately, many women have felt bound to violent relationships because of the understanding of these passages gained from sermons and admonitions in the past—as well as pastoral exhortations and "holy cards" they may have received during an abuse experience. In your own attempts to live up to what you perceived as the requirements of your faith, you may have lived in constant fear for your life and well-being. Fear and dread do not constitute the role you or anyone else should have in a family.

The Sanctity of Marriage

Churches and synagogues have long held enviable reputations for maintaining the sanctity of marriage and the family. They have often been the almost solitary bastions for the values of loyalty and commitment within the family. They have upheld marriage as a sacred and permanent covenant.

The roots of such a role and responsibility are found in the creation story. Adam and Eve are formed from a common flesh and are urged to cling to one another and become one flesh (Gen. 2:23–24). Together they shared the beauties of the garden and together they suffered the results of their common failure.

The Mosaic covenant, which brought the Israelites together as the people of God, also affirmed the importance of the family as the basic unit of the new nation. Many of the regulations promulgated to preserve the new community focused on the family (see especially Lev. 20:9–21). Many of the decisions made regarding the distribution of the wealth found in their new land flowing with milk and honey were made according to family grouping. In fact, much of the book of Joshua details this distribution through use of the recurring phrase "according to the family of . . . ."

Since the family is both the basic social unit of any community and the principal source of nurture and support for members of the community, especially its children, it is critical that the family be permanent and stable. It is important that the relationship upon which the family is based not easily be "separated." It is understandable that the prophet Malachi would proclaim, " 'For I hate divorce,' says the Lord God of Israel" (2:16). It would make sense for Paul to say, "To the married I give this command—not I but the Lord—that the wife should not separate from her husband . . . and that the husband should not divorce his wife" (1 Cor. 7:10–11) and "A wife is bound as long as her husband lives" (1 Cor. 7:39). Such admonitions make good sense for society as well as sound spiritual direction.

When we consider the important role that the family has in the formation of children and in establishing the spiritual climate of a society we can appreciate the importance of the Rabbinic concept of *shalom bayit*, "peace in the household," or domestic tranquillity, as a goal to be sought in every family in order to foster the proper nurturing of its members.

No one would deny or minimize the important role of the family. As a battered woman you may have subjected yourself to considerable pain and anguish in an effort to preserve your family. However, the fact of family violence and particularly the spouse abuse, which you know so well, demands that we look closely at what we consider the essence of a family and what truly constitutes a marriage.

A key characteristic of marriage in the Hebrew and Christian traditions is faithfulness. The prophet Malachi does not merely proclaim God's displeasure with divorce. He goes on to counsel, "So take heed to yourselves and do not be faithless" (2:16). Jesus' admonition about divorce is made in the context of his concern for the misuse of divorce proceedings for reasons other than unfaithfulness. Paul's advice to married couples is intended to encourage equal and willing partners who are experiencing difficulties to seek every possible source of reconciliation.

None of these scriptural admonitions insist that marriages be maintained in the face of threats to life and limb for one of the members. Most interpreters of the Jewish and Christian traditions have allowed that special circumstances, most notably the unfaithfulness that has destroyed the basis of a relationship, provide grounds for ending a marriage. The most common "unfaithfulness" thought to justify divorce is adultery. However, if you have experienced battering, you might want to ask whether family violence is not also a form of unfaithfulness. Did not the abuse that threatened your life or health constitute a violation of your marriage covenant? It certainly went a long way toward destroying the trust upon which your marriage relationship ought to have been based. As Marie Fortune has put it, "If you can't trust your husband not to hit you, what can you trust?" (1987, 34).

The reality is that the abuse you experienced in your marriage was probably more destructive to your relationship than adultery would have been. It was certainly more devastating to your children whom your family was supposed to be nurturing and protecting. Your children were likely more aware of violence between you and your spouse than of sexual infidelities on the part of either of you. They also were more threatened by the violence because they frequently may have wondered whether the next blows would be directed at them—and if your family was like many violent families, they often were.

The unity of marriage is an ideal to be sought. No one should "separate" the relationship between persons committed to one another in marriage. However, as anyone who has lived in an abusive relationship knows, that admonition not to separate must be addressed not only to the battered wife who seeks shelter and counsel about her options. That admonition should be addressed primarily to her abusive husband who has already severed the relationship through his violence.

The same principle applies to the ideal of *shalom bayit*. To accuse a battered wife of destroying domestic tranquility when she speaks up about the violence she is experiencing is comparable to accusing Jews who complained about the death camps in Nazi Germany of being unpatriotic. The peace in the household already was destroyed weeks, months, and often years before when the cycle of violence began. When you as a battered woman sought help, you were trying to reestablish truth and integrity (essential elements of *shalom*) in your life. You were attempting to put peace back into your life and the lives of your children. As Rabbi Julie Spitzer puts it, "*Sh'lom Bayit* must be held up as an ideal—not as a trap, but as a release. Keeping peace in the home is not a reason to stay in an abusive situation. It is a reason to leave one" (1985, 51). Once the cycle of violence is broken (usually by outside counseling intervention), then it is possible to consider whether the process of rebuilding domestic tranquility is a possibility. And it may not be. The peace of the household may be too fractured, the trust too crushed.

If you experienced abuse in your marriage, you recognize that spousal violence undermines the sanctity of marriage and the stability that marriage is supposed to bring to society. You know that only when violence has been eradicated from a marriage can that union be said to be truly holy.

Guided Meditations for Survivors

The following guided meditations are offered as models of the kinds of meditations recommended in chapter 8. They are intended only as suggestions to get you started. They have been written with the specific needs of survivors of abuse in mind. Do not think that you have to use all of each meditation at any one time. Go as far as is comfortable for you. Stop whenever time or tension tells you that you have gone far enough. I am indebted to Eddie Ensley and his book, *Prayer That Heals Our Emotions*, for the model employed for these meditations. I recommend the meditations in his book as an additional resource.

Prayer of Light

Sit comfortably, relax, and be still. Focus your eyes or your mind's eye on a source of light. You might choose a flame, the soft light of a lamp, or the sun itself. Experience the warmth and glow that that light can give. Let yourself be surrounded by that light so your whole body is warmed and soothed.

As you experience that light, remember that God in the act of creation was the source of light and that God's love enlightens our lives and can eliminate the darkness of fear and anger. Let the light of God's love surround and fill your body, your mind, and your heart. Gently let the light of God's love illuminate the parts of your mind and body that have been injured by your abuse. Let yourself rest in that light. Relax in the soothing warmth of the light of God.

If you wish to go further, as you rest in the glow you feel, begin to be aware of your breathing. Note how you breathe in and how you breathe out. Know that in creation God breathed life into the first humans. As you inhale, breathe in the warmth of God, the clarifying brightness of God's love. Breathe in light, warmth, and healing. Breathe out darkness, pain, and fear. Let the spirit of God, which you breathe in, warm and soothe the center of your body and let it flow from the center into other parts of your body. Let it gently filter into the parts of your body afflicted by abuse—your arms, legs, shoulders, genitals—caressing, soothing, warming, affirming, releasing. Feel the healing power of God's light in your body and your whole life. Remain in this soothing light as long as you like.

Prayer of Emptying

(This meditation is for a time when you are anxious and full of fear, when frightening images and flashbacks are dominating your life. Do not attempt this meditation alone. Invite a friend to be with you or at least nearby.)

Sit comfortably, relax as much as you can, and be still. Invite God to be with you. Visualize God's presence as a warm light, using the light images from the meditation above, or as soothing water that caresses your body. Bathed in God's presence, instead of trying to block the memories and images that have been assailing you, choose one on which to focus. Feeling God's caring and protective presence try to remember as many details as possible of the incident you are remembering. Recall the feelings you had at the time. Let the tension and fear of that moment permeate your body, fill every muscle and joint. Let your body-memories of the abuse event surface and flood your body.

Now invite God to help you overcome the fear and tension that have been trying to rule your body. Begin with your extremities, your head, hands, and feet. Focus the light of God or God's soothing water on each of those parts of your body. Let the light/water warm, soothe, and caress your extremities, washing out or evaporating the fear and tension. Let the light/water pull out the tension, wash out the fear. Feel it seep out through your toes and finger tips, the top of your head. Watch the memories—and with them your anxiety and tension—evaporate as steam in the heat of the light and be washed away in the flowing stream.

When your fingers and toes, hands and feet are relaxed and soothed, let the light/water move on to the next part of your body, your arms, legs, neck, and shoulders. Let the light/water work on each part of your body until the tension and fear, the body-memories related to the abuse incident you are remembering, dissipate and evaporate in the warmth and caress of God's love. Repeat this process with every part of your body, taking special care to soothe and relieve those parts of your body most seriously injured by the abuse.

When you have let God's love soothe your whole body, take as much time as you like to revel in God's loving embrace. Then return to your room relieved of some of your anxieties.

APPENDIX C
Psalms
by a Survivor

The following are taken from a collection of contemporary lamentation psalms written by a survivor after reading parts of this book manuscript (the numbering is from her collection). She found that studying the psalms allowed her to express in prayer her own anger at God.

Psalm 2—Punish My Abusers

God of hope and of all blessings,
    I need your help and assurance.

My tormentors have walked free,
    While I have been racked with pain.

Where is my freedom?
    Where is their punishment?

I have worked with much difficulty,
    Fear, doubt, and trepidation to recover.

Where is their punishment? Why do they walk free?
    You speak of justice. Where is your wrath upon them?

I ask for your wrath upon those who brought me down,
    They took me to the bottom of their wretchedness,
        They took me to their lowliness with them.

I have been brought low, to the bottom of the pit,
    Where I was tortured. Then, I was abandoned there.

Where is your justice? Where is your wrath for them?
  Your punishment to them will show me my innocence.

I did no wrong in infancy, and yet I was abused.
  Why do you not show me your disgust at them?

Give them the pain of memories which seem unbelievable,
  As I have had to face, to reach to the other side.

Give them the pain of guilt for their behavior,
  Give them full experience of their faculties
    Which through their trickery, they have blocked.

Give them accountability for their actions,
  Allow them full shame for their actions to me.

Give them the pain of full recovery,
  Allow them to struggle to change the persons
    Which they have allowed themselves to become.

Grant them torment in their memories, to utter confusion,
  To grief beyond their understanding.

Sentence them to perfection in their recovery
  As they have had in their torturous behavior
    Thus far in their lives.

Sentence them to rigorous rituals to undo their actions,
  Allow them to know the number of times of their abuse.

Allow them to understand the depths of the pit of hell,
  Be sure they understand abandonment, shame.

Let them, oh God, feel the vastness of emptiness
  Of not knowing who they are, because they can please no one,
    No matter how hard they try.

Inflict upon them the experience of total shame
  For being who they are, their presence.

Be sure they know the destruction of being attacked for
  Failing to die under their abuse to the point of torture.

Oh God, who I believe will affirm me in my righteousness,
  Regarding these issues, your punishment
    Will fit their crime.

Oh God, of mercy and of love, I also believe
  In your justice and raising up of the downtrodden.
    I believe, I trust, I hope, and in waiting I thank you.
Amen.

Psalm 4—I Chose You

I felt as if thrown down into a pit,
    An endless pit. You were watching for I knew,
        "You know all things." Where were you, God?

I was falling and you had not come,
    You had not come to carry me into your loving,
        Your everlasting arms to peace, acceptance.

I kept falling, there was no one to catch me.
    My soul cried out for saving. "Bring me up!"
        Why did you not pluck me up, oh God?

I kept falling down, down into the bottomless pit.
    The depths of their evil astounded me,
        You did not save this little one.

I was so small when they took me over,
    I was pulled down, down, down, into the dungeons,
        I was helpless, alone, afraid.

Where were you, oh God of hope, understanding?
    You said, "Do not hurt the little ones."
        Yes, God, but God, where were you?

I had no power, no strength against them,
    I was small and you let them overpower me.
        I was an infant and even then, it was you whom I chose.

I was so overcome by their size, by their power over me,
    And even then, in my smallness,
        Yes, even in my infancy, I chose you!

Where were you, God? Their robes and candles were used,
    Their trickery did not fool me.
        I know they were not you. Where were you, God?

They used chant and ritual to fool me.
    I knew better. I had chosen you.
        In the smallness of my infancy I chose you.

I chose you before I knew my choosing.
    I chose you from before I learned choice.
        I always believed, always hoped.

You said You were the God of the universe,
    Were you the God of the people within it?
        Were you not the one who frees us from abandonment?

I was abandoned, frightened, helpless, alone,
  Where were you, God? I needed you,
    You were not to be found.

In my loneliness, my heart sank.
  Why did you hide your face from me?
    What offense had I done to you?

My accusers had taught me guilt. Did you accuse me also?
  They cloaked me, wrapped me in their shame.
    What offense had I done to you?

I was still alive and my hope did not fail me,
  I struggled, I survived, my hope continued,
    I had no hope, but hope. Only my hope held me.
Amen.

Psalm 5—All of Me

Oh God of creation and perfect order, I believe in you,
  I make a plea to you to hear my supplication,
    For healing: mind, emotion, body, spirit.

My captors have gotten to every part of my being,
  Yes, every portion, every cell of me.
    Every part attacked, disarranged, distraught.

I have been held at knife point, frightened and afraid.
  I was tied and gagged. Where were you?
    In the silence of my mind I called for you.

I was left naked, cold, damp. I was unprotected, shamed.
  I had no one to turn to. Where were you?
    I longed to be covered, to be held.

I was raped, tormented by one and another, another and more.
  My captors were beyond me in age, weight, strength.
    Why were you not saving me?

I was covered with needles throughout my flesh.
  My captors removed blood from me.
    Why did you not come to take me away?

My body so lifeless and unprotected,
  Were you not, oh God, the maker of every cell in me?
    Why was I attacked, desecrated?

My mind was racked with unbelief,
   Because the ordinariness of the day
      Defied the terror of the night.

In my dreams came nightmares, wet dreams followed.
   In reporting my dreams I was told of my imagination.
      I was disbelieved. I was told I lied.

My mind went through torment, trying to discern
   The real from the unreal. Confusion reigned.
      My captors used tricks to fool me.

My feelings came, but I was forbidden to feel.
   Only rage was permitted. Forbidden to feel.
      Rage and anger reserved for men and boys.

I could not feel anything at the appropriate time.
   I was all ice inside, shut down. At happy times
      I could not feel. When sad, I laughed, hysteria.

My spirit was desecrated, as my body, mind, emotion.
   My spirit wept, waiting for you. Where were you? Oh God,
      My spirit sank, with no hope of ever finding you
         again.

And today, oh God, I still beg understanding.
   I know not why you abandoned me.
      Where is your mercy, your love?

I am grateful for the end to the actual pain of it.
   But for years I lamented living it over, over again.
      Convincing myself that I was not crazy.

Today the torment of all the pointless agony
   Continues to astound me. Why, oh God,
      Why have you forsaken me?

I was small, innocent, alone and I was defenseless.
   With no one to turn to, all I could do was turn inward.
      But inward I used my strength and did not turn bitter.

Within I found the stuff of which I am made
   And found there in the caverns of my mind,
      My own saving grace.

I am grateful for the gift I found and developed for myself.
   Inside of me was a gift to give to some forgetting part
      The pain which I had endured.

My gift worked and saved me. I had a secret which
  No one could remove from me. I hid within myself
    Where no one could find me.

In the caverns of my mind I was able to save my soul,
  But not my emotions, nor my flesh. All of me ached.
    Where did you hide your comfort from me?

Surviving I await your comfort, oh God.
  In my frustration and agony I await to hear from you.
    Come to me and hold me and I will cry,
  Cry tears of joy.
Amen.

Bibliography

This bibliography contains not only works cited in this book but also several that the author considers important resources for further understanding of survivor issues and growth in spirituality for survivors. It does not claim to be comprehensive, only a beginning guide for further reading.

Bass, Ellen, and Laura Davis. *The Courage to Heal: A Guide for Women Survivors of Child Sexual Abuse*. New York: Harper & Row, 1988.

Bingham, Carol Findon, ed. *Doorway to Response: The Role of Clergy in Ministry with Battered Women*. Illinois Conference Churches, 1986.

Birnbaum, Philip. *Maimonides' Mishneh Torah*. New York: Hebrew Publishing Co., 1967.

Blumenthal, David R. *Facing the Abusing God*. Louisville, Ky.: Westminster/John Knox Press, 1993.

———. Letter to author, 12 November 1990.

Bradshaw, John. *Healing the Shame That Binds You*. Deerfield, Fla.: Health Communications, 1988.

Brown, J. C., and C. R. Bohn. *Christianity, Patriarchy and Abuse: A Feminist Critique*. New York: Pilgrim Press, 1989.

Brueggemann, Walter. *Finally Comes the Poet*. Minneapolis: Fortress Press, 1989.

———. *Hope Within History*. Atlanta: John Knox Press, 1987.

175

———. "Hurt and Hope: When Power Overrides Pain." Hiram Lecture, Hiram College Lecture Series, Hiram, Ohio, delivered 23 April 1991.

———. *The Message of the Psalms*. Minneapolis: Augsburg Publishing House, 1984.

Bussert, Joy M. K. *Battered Women: From a Theology of Suffering to an Ethic of Empowerment*. New York: Division for Mission in North America, Lutheran Church in America, 1986.

Children's Defense Fund. *A Call for Action to Make Our Nation Safe for Children*. Washington, D.C.: Children's Defense Fund, 1988.

Clarke, Rita-Lou. *Pastoral Care of Battered Women*. Philadelphia: Westminster Press, 1986.

Coffin, William Sloane, Speech delivered to the Eighth Annual Assembly of the World YMCA, Geneva, 1981.

Collins, Sheila. *A Different Heaven and Earth*. Valley Forge, Pa.: Judson Press, 1974.

Courtois, Christine A. *Healing the Incest Wound: Adult Survivors in Therapy*. New York: W. W. Norton & Co., 1988.

Daugherty, Lynn B. *Why Me? Help for Victims of Child Sexual Abuse (Even If They Are Adults Now)*. Racine, Wis.: Mother Courage Press, 1984.

DelBane, Ron. *The Breath of Life: A Simple Way to Pray*. Minneapolis: Winston Press, 1981.

Diagnostic and Statistical Manual, Vol. III. Washington, D.C.: American Psychiatric Association, 1980.

Dobash, R. Emerson, and Russell Dobash. *Violence Against Wives: A Case Against the Patriarchy*. New York: Macmillan Publishing Co., 1979.

Ensley, Eddie. *Prayer That Heals Our Emotions*. San Francisco: Harper & Row, 1988.

Erikson, E. H. *Childhood and Society*. New York: W. W. Norton & Co., 1963.

Fortune, Marie M. *Is Nothing Sacred? When Sex Invades the Pastoral Relationship*. San Francisco: Harper & Row, 1989.

———. *Keeping the Faith: Questions and Answers for the Abused*. New York: Harper & Row, 1987.

————. "Making Justice: Sources of Healing for Incest Survivors." *Working Together* 7, no. 4 (1988): 5, 6.

————. *Sexual Violence: The Unmentionable Sin.* New York: Pilgrim Press, 1983.

Foster, Richard J. *Celebration of Discipline: The Path to Spiritual Growth.* San Francisco: Harper & Row, 1988.

Fox, Matthew. *Original Blessing.* Santa Fe, N.M.: Bear, 1983.

Garbarino, James, and Gwen Gilliam. *Understanding Abusive Families.* Lexington, Mass.: D.C. Heath & Co., 1980.

Gelles, Richard J. *Family Violence.* Beverly Hills, Calif.: Sage Publications, 1979.

————, and Claire Pedrick Cornell. *Intimate Violence in Families.* Beverly Hills, Calif.: Sage Publications, 1985.

Goldbrunner, Josef. *Holiness Is Wholeness.* Notre Dame, Ind.: University of Notre Dame, 1964.

Green, Bonnie L.; John P. Wilson; and Jacob D. Lindy. "A Conceptual Framework for Post-Traumatic Stress Syndromes Among Survivor Groups." Paper presented at the Thirty-third annual meeting of the Institute on Hospital and Community Psychiatry, San Diego, September 1981.

Greven, Philip. *The Protestant Temperament: Patterns of Child-Rearing, Religious Experience, and the Self in Early America.* New York: Alfred A. Knopf, 1977.

Harrison, Beverly Wildung. *Making the Connections: Essays in Feminist Social Ethics.* Boston: Beacon Press, 1985.

Helfer, Ray E. *Childhood Comes First: A Crash Course in Childhood for Adults.* East Lansing, Mich.: Helfer, 1984.

Hyde, Margaret O. *Cry Softly! The Story of Child Abuse.* Philadelphia: Westminster Press, 1986.

Johnson, David, and Jeff VanVonderen. *The Subtle Power of Spiritual Abuse.* Minneapolis: Bethany House Publishers, 1991.

Justice, Blair, and Rita Justice. *The Abusing Family.* New York: Human Sciences Press, 1976.

Kushner, Harold S. *When Bad Things Happen to Good People.* New York: Avon Books, 1981.

Laytner, Anson. *Arguing with God: A Jewish Tradition.* Northvale, N.J.: Jason Aronson, 1990.

Leaman, Karen M. "Sexual Abuse: The Reactions of Child and Family", *Sexual Abuse of Children: Selected Readings.* Washington, D.C.: U.S. Department of Health and Human Services, 1980.

Lechman, Judith C. *Yielding to Courage: The Spiritual Path to Overcoming Fear.* San Francisco: Harper & Row, 1988.

Leehan, James. *Pastoral Care for Survivors of Family Abuse.* Louisville, Ky.: Westminster/John Knox Press, 1989.

Leehan, James, and Laura Wilson. *Grown-Up Abused Children.* Springfield, Ill.: Charles C. Thomas Publishers, 1985.

LeShan, Lawrence. *How to Meditate.* New York: Bantam, 1974.

Lester, Andrew D. *Coping with Your Anger: A Christian Guide.* Philadelphia: Westminster Press, 1983.

Lew, Mike. *Victims No Longer: Men Recovering from Incest and Other Sexual Child Abuse.* New York: Harper & Row, 1990.

maiz, b. f. *Dear Stranger.* Fort Worth, Tex.: Tuff Co., 1978.

Martin, Del. *Battered Wives.* San Francisco: Glide Publications, 1976.

Maslow, Abraham H. *Motivation and Personality.* New York: Harper & Row, 1987.

Merton, Thomas. *Contemplative Prayer.* New York: Herder & Herder, 1969.

Miller, Alice. *Breaking Down the Wall of Silence.* New York: E. P. Dutton, 1991.

Montefiore, C. G., and H. Loewe. *A Rabbinic Anthology.* Cleveland: World Publishing Co., 1963.

Nouwen, Henri J. M. *Reaching Out: The Three Movements of the Spiritual Life.* Garden City, N.Y.: Doubleday & Co., 1975.

———. *The Wounded Healer: Ministry in Contemporary Society.* Garden City, N.Y.: Doubleday & Co., 1972.

Price-Martin, Barbara. "Theological Reflections on the Religious Dimension in Family Violence." *Working Together* 6, no. 3 (1987): 2–4.

Richardson, Alan, ed. *A Theological Word Book of the Bible.* New York: Macmillan Co., 1950.

Sanford, Linda T. *Strong at the Broken Places*. New York: Avon, 1990.

Simon, Sidney, and Suzanne Simon. *Forgiveness*. New York: Warner Books, 1990.

Smedes, Lewis B. *Forgive and Forget: Healing the Hurts We Don't Deserve*. New York: Pocket Books, 1986. This book is helpful despite its unfortunate title.

Spitzer, Julie Ringold. *Spousal Abuse in Rabbinic and Contemporary Judaism*. New York: National Federation of Temple Sisterhoods, 1987.

Steinmetz, Suzanne K. *The Cycle of Violence*. New York: Praeger Publishers, 1977.

Stettbacher, J. Konrad. *Making Sense of Suffering: The Healing Confrontation with your Past*. New York: E. P. Dutton & Co., 1991.

Straus, Murray A.; Gelles, Richard J.; Steinmetz, Suzanne K. *Behind Closed Doors: Violence in the American Family*. Garden City, N.Y.: Anchor Books, 1980.

Tavris, Carol. *Anger: The Misunderstood Emotion*. New York: Simon & Schuster, 1982.

Tillich, Paul. *The Courage To Be*. New Haven, Conn.: Yale University Press, 1952.

Trible, Phyllis. *God and the Rhetoric of Sexuality*. Philadelphia: Fortress Press, 1978.

Walker, Lenore. *The Battered Woman*. New York: Harper & Row, 1979.

Wink, Walter. "Prayer and the Powers." *Sojourners* 19 (October 1990): 10–14.

Wood, Frances E. "Mandatory 'Niceness': An Impediment to Justice and the Healing Process." *Working Together* 7, no. 6 (1988): 1, 2.